The Iraq War Blog

*An Iraqi Family's Inside View of the
First Year of the Occupation*

Faiza Al-Araji, Raed Jarrar, and Khalid Jarrar

Foreword by
Steve Connors and Molly Bingham
Directors, *Meeting Resistance*

Nashville, Tennessee

Nashville, Tennessee
www.secondchancepublishing.com
info@secondchancepublishing.com

The Iraq War Blog © 2008 by Faiza Al-Araji, Raed Jarrar, and Khalid Jarrar

Foreword © 2008 by Steve Connors and Molly Bingham

Cover design by Love It! Designs

ISBN 0-9716795-0-9

Library of Congress Control Number: 2008930190

The Iraq War Blog

*An Iraqi Family's Inside View of the
First Year of the Occupation*

Faiza Al-Araji, Raed Jarrar, and Khalid Jarrar

Foreword by
Steve Connors and Molly Bingham
Directors, *Meeting Resistance*

To the people of Iraq...

"My belief is we will, in fact, be greeted as liberators."
— VICE PRESIDENT DICK CHENEY, "MEET THE PRESS,"
MARCH 16, 2003

ACKNOWLEDGEMENTS

Our deepest thanks go to Michael DeFilippo at Second Chance Publishing for initiating this project, and for his dedication and patience. This book project would not have been possible without him.

We are grateful to May in Baghdad, Candid, Manal, Riverbend, Mohammed in Egypt, and Diaa Hadid in Dubai for translating Faiza's blog into English, and to my wife, Niki, for helping to edit our blogs along the way.

We would like to extend our thanks to Liza Hippler of Love It! Designs for the excellent work she did on the cover and the layout of the book.

We would personally wish to thank you, our readers, for taking the time to learn more about the occupation of Iraq.

Finally, we are thankful to Google™ for the free blogging space.

i

In 2003, we began the reporting for our documentary, *Meeting Resistance*. Over a period of ten months, we interviewed Iraqis who violently oppose the occupation of their country by American and coalition forces. We were immediately struck by how different their stories were from the descriptions being put out by the United States military that were being repeated by the Western media.

Contrary to the official reports that the nascent, armed resistance was made up of criminals, former regime elements, and people on the fringes of Iraqi society, we were finding that they were mostly ordinary people, some of whom had taken up arms for the first time, fighting to maintain their independence and national self-determination. But it wasn't just history's first draft that was in dispute—it was almost everything we thought we knew about Iraq. With each passing day, it became increasingly clear to us that in the decade leading up to the war an entire alternative narrative about Iraq had been constructed by an assortment of exile groups, politicians and commentators of different stripes, each projecting their own version of Iraq to suit their agenda.

From mobile chemical weapons laboratories to mass graves containing hundreds of thousands, "facts" only needed repeating often enough to become true. We had all taken it on faith that the Iraqi people were largely secular (but with the unquestioned contradiction that the *Shi'a* had been oppressed for reasons of religious bigotry) and that our forces would be greeted as liberators by a grateful, downtrodden population, eager for Western style democracy and social freedoms. Well, that's what we were told and without information to the contrary what else could we do but accept the lie? Until, that is, thousands of journalists from all over the world descended on the country and began digging for more reliable, first-hand knowledge.

But that didn't happen. Of course, the journalists came, but there was little interest in tearing down the wall of deceit and disinformation. Instead, construction of the edifice continued apace and in a complicit manner a significant portion the worlds' media went along with it. Soon the telling of the tale had become such a distortion of reality that the people of Iraq no longer recognized themselves as part of the subject under discussion. And there was worse to come. As the occupiers struggled from crisis to crisis, they began to create a surface semblance to the Iraq they had portrayed. In seeking to avoid a unified anti-occupation front, the American military and diplomatic teams sought to exploit divisions in Iraq by setting family against family, tribe against tribe, and sect against sect. In both the military operations and political chicanery, all that really mattered were the interests of the United States. The consequences for Iraq and its people were rarely considered, or only considered as how it could be spun "at home."

We're now in the sixth year of the *Iraq War*—or the *American War* if you're Iraqi—and the situation seems quite hopeless. But if we are willing to face reality, we'll find that "ancient sectarian hatreds" are not so old, that reconciliation is an ongoing process, and that unity, not division, is the paradigm of Iraq. That may be a terrifying prospect for an occupying power, heavily invested in having its own way, but it is also a reality that no amount of historical revisionism has yet been able to dislodge.

So, where can we find that reality of Iraq? The Iraqis who have spent the last thirty years in Iraq rather than in exile can testify to this reality and there is no better place to begin than with this compilation of blog posts by Faiza Al-Ajari and her sons, Raed and Khalid. Faiza opens with *Shock and Awe* but she doesn't call it that, because remember, she's telling us about *America's War* and happens to be on the receiving end. In those first few days, when the attacking nations raised the flag and celebrated the prowess of our military machines, Faiza just tells us how it feels; she's terrified and with good reason. For all the talk of "surgical strikes" against "high value targets," Faiza reminds us just who paid the price of "liberation."

The looting of Baghdad has been analyzed time and time again in the partisan bickering that has sought to apportion blame for what went wrong in Iraq. Were there enough troops? Were they properly trained? Faiza sees it differently. "The American tanks are roaming the streets, but they are not concerned with the killings or lootings, they do not interfere. What are they doing then?" she says, then goes on to scold the glib cruelty of the architect of all this chaos and pain. "Rumsfeld said that freedom is chaotic, and people are free to commit crimes and do bad things. I don't understand how these people think! Do they live like this in America? People killing, looting, and committing all sins. Is this really *The Freedom*?"

So it continues as Faiza and her sons take us back along a road we believe we have already traveled. But now, with these guides, we are directed to a new way of seeing. As we pass through a landscape not quite familiar because of the shift in viewpoint, we become aware that our discovery is so much more than a revisiting of events. We begin to see the signposts of a people, their history, and their culture. Small, personal revelations become pointers to greater meaning, understanding follows exposition, and finally we find ourselves in a place and context from where we can begin to understand where it is we truly stand as a people, and what it is that the Iraqis have since those first days. They looked furtively for signs that the freedom delivered them would be wonderful. But it is with increased bitterness that they recognize that the show of force, the gathering of nations, the advancing army, the overthrow of the dictator, the words of liberty and democracy thrown down as gauntlets—that none of this was really done for them. And through reading these daily thoughts as the days of the invasion and occupation passed, we as westerners can glimpse the source of the bitterness that the Iraqis taste.

Steve Connors & Molly Bingham
Directors, *Meeting Resistance*
April 2008

Introduction

During the early months after the 2003 invasion of Iraq, sources for reliable information on the impact of the war were few and far between. The mainstream U.S. media, which had blindly and uncritically participated in the Bush administration's drumbeat for war, certainly could not be trusted. Self-described "embedded" journalists on the ground produced militarized and military perspectives of the war as pundits on U.S. airwaves, who knew neither the language nor history of Iraq, claimed to provide "expert" analysis.

In this barren landscape, the blogs of the Jarrar brothers and their mother Faiza Al-Araji were a welcome respite from the relentless barrage of misinformation. Writing from three very different perspectives and each with their own unique style, the blogs all captured the devastating consequences of the war for a family and country that had already lived through over a decade of debilitating sanctions and air raids.

Faiza Al-Araji's detailed postings on the blog, *A Family in Baghdad*, chronicled the daily impact of the war with candor and emotion, the way one might write in a private diary. This candid quality lent the blog an intimacy absent in almost all of the coverage of the Iraq war: the reader was allowed into the lives of the family via the writings of a working mother deeply concerned about the fate of her children and country. Even the reader with little political inclinations could relate to the worries Faiza shared with her audience.

Writing first in the joint blog, *Where is Raed?*, and later moving onto his own site, *Raed in the Middle*, Raed Jarrar provided information about developments in Iraq along with incisive political analysis. Witty and straightforward, Raed never played to the gallery. Whether or not his audience was ready or willing to face the ugly realities of occupied Iraq, Raed laid them out for us. Fully in grasp of the internal dynamics of the country, Raed also offered solutions and predictions of what would happen if those options were not followed.

The more playful blog of the three, Khalid's *Secrets in Baghdad*, managed to convey the harsh consequences of the war while including lighthearted entries about his daily interactions with friends and readers. A university student at the time of the invasion, Khalid's blog often addressed the impact of the war on campus life: jumpy students who easily startle at the slightest sound, teachers having to cancel classes out of concern for security, and a series of other emergency disruptions that deprive Khalid and his classmates of a normal education, much less a fun college life.

In short, the Jarrar brothers and their mother, Faiza Al-Araji, provided what the mainstream U.S. media rarely showed: real Iraqis and real news about Iraq. It seemed that blogs held the key to gaining reliable insight into the conduct of the war and the situation on the ground. Yet even in those days, there were signs that the blogosphere too was becoming just another site for the dissemination of propaganda. Alongside the blogs of Faiza, Raed, Khalid, and a few other Iraqis who wrote openly and honestly about the situation, there appeared a handful of other sites that parroted the official narratives of the Bush administration.

While these sites claimed to be the blogs of ordinary Iraqis, they were curiously linked to a number of other Web sites and organizations hardly known in Iraq or the region, but well established in the U.S. as proponents of a particular ideology that had paved the way to a war on Iraq. Unlike the Jarrar brothers and their mother, who shared their full names, photos of themselves and their home, these bloggers only provided generic sounding first names and very vague information about their backgrounds. For reasons about which one can only speculate, these pro-war "Iraqi" blogs also received widespread attention from mainstream outlets and institutions, which promoted them as "authentic" voices of the Iraqi people. Even in those early days, there were signs that the blogosphere was being co-opted.

More than five years after the 2003 invasion, the Iraqi blogosphere has expanded. Sadly, the blogging phenomenon overall, rather than being the domain of independent voices, is increasingly turning into yet another echo chamber for dominant narratives about Iraq and the Iraq war. Blogs such as those of the Jarrars and their mother is now in the minority, while one often comes across the sites of Iraqis who are pro-war, who work with the U.S. military in various capacities, or merely repeat whatever cliché the corporate U.S. media or administration is entertaining on a particular day.

What this book captures is an historical moment in two senses. On the one hand, it reveals the destructive consequences of the U.S. war on Iraq from the point of view of three members of an ordinary Iraqi family. In addition, it captures a moment in time when the blogosphere still had room for independent voices to be heard.

Niki Akhavan, Ph.D
May 2008

The Iraq War Blog

TUESDAY, MARCH 18, 2003

Today, George W. Bush gave Saddam Hussein forty-eight hours to leave Iraq or face war.

Although everyone in the city went to work today, the atmosphere is depressing and the smell of war is all over the place. Already Baghdad is preparing for war. The streets are full of sandbags for fighting positions and there are huge holes in the ground full of burning oil to prevent the American fighters from seeing the city clearly. People are running to collect food and other important things before hiding in their houses; everyone is trying to see their friends and family before going to hide. Who can tell? Maybe this will be the last time we meet.

Every Iraqi house is stocked with food rations: rice, sugar, flour, beans, canned vegetables, juices, and mineral water. There is also soap, laundry detergent, toilet paper, petrol for the cars, and diesel for the generators. Most houses have wells in their backyards.

On my way home today, I went to a small greenhouse and bought ten flowering plants in different colors and shapes. I decided to enjoy life until the last moment. I want to drive around Baghdad to say good-bye. Maybe some parts of Baghdad will disappear. I also want to see the Tigris River before the war begins.

Raed, my oldest son went out to visit his friends and had my car keys in his pocket, so I could not drive around Baghdad tonight. I felt very bad, so I just went to visit my neighbors to have some chai, and speak about the war and what everyone is expecting. I came back home feeling alienated and anxious. But there is one thing that comforts me: Raed is with us. *Alhamdu lellah* (thanks to God) that the whole family is together. If Raed was in Amman now he would be worried about us, and we would be worried about him.

Faiza Al-Araji

WEDNESDAY, MARCH 19, 2003

I spent the day doing some housework, washing clothes, and cleaning the kitchen. I didn't work today; instead, we evacuated our showrooms. They looked so sad and empty. All the shops are closed, the streets are empty, and the houses are full of families and relatives who left their unsafe homes. Some families even fled Baghdad and some left the country altogether.

It's very quiet outside, but the silence is reassuring. I can almost hear the city saying, "You'll miss me." I am uncomfortable because of the unexpected change in our daily schedule: no school, no work, no leaving the house. I'm not even sure that I feel like reading a book.

I had a dream a few days ago. I was standing in a large green garden and in middle of the garden, there was a house. Around the garden there was a fence, a part of which was broken. Suddenly, a long yellow snake slithered out from the broken part. It came around the house and people ran away from the house. Then some smaller snakes came out of the big one and hid behind the bushes. On the roof of the house, I saw some leaking water tanks and men trying to fix them to protect us from the falling water. Then I saw all of us in a safe house. We saw a black dog approaching and he seemed to be very tired. I felt sad and asked what was wrong with the dog? I was told that his sons were taken from him.

My neighbor says that maybe this dream symbolizes Saddam and his sons and that this could be their end. A snake in a dream signifies an enemy, and perhaps my dream means that Iraq is going to be occupied.

I remember what my father used to say: "Who takes the chair (authority) with blood, won't leave it except with blood."

Faiza Al-Araji

THURSDAY, MARCH 20, 2003

After dawn prayer, we heard sirens, and the first attack started. I ran to the cellar, where I made breakfast and the family ate together.

Our family is lucky because we have a hidden satellite receiver on which we watched the news channels. We learned that everyone in the world was watching us. The bombing was far way, so it didn't seem to be dangerous; maybe it would be more dangerous in the days to come. We heard on the news that this is just the beginning, and the next attack will be huge.

The evening bombing lasted for more than an hour. I could clearly hear the sounds of the missiles, and the anti-aircraft guns. My stomach hurts and I feel depressed. How many days is it going to be like this? We are like prisoners. Wars are a silly way to solve problems. When will life return to normal?

Faiza Al-Araji

SATURDAY, MARCH 22, 2003

Last night was a disaster. The missile attacks were so huge that they shook houses and broke windows. The room was shaking; the curtains blew in the air after every missile exploded, and there were just a few seconds between one missile and the next. Now we can see the ugly face of war.

We went through some very terrifying moments. I covered my face with my hands and read some verses from the Qur'an. I was frightened to death! When the bombings seemed further away, I took a sleeping pill. Azzam went to prepare dinner, but I refused to leave the room. Our whole family sleeps in one room, in the deepest part of our house, far from the street. We call it our safe room. Most of the other families have safe rooms too, where they sleep together. We had our dinner in the same room, and I slept on the floor.

I woke up at Athan (announcement) of dawn prayer and I could still hear explosions far away, and all the mosques praying and

3

repeating *Allaho Akbar, Allaho Akbar.* (God is the greatest.) My soul felt secure and safe; I finished my *Wodooa* (washing before praying) and prayed.

Then sirens were screaming again announcing the beginning of a new attack. In the early morning, many of our relatives phoned us. *Hamdella As Salama, Hamdella As Salama* (appreciation to God for our safety). It seems that everyone heard on the news that bombing was near our neighborhood last night.

Faiza Al-Araji

SUNDAY, MARCH 23, 2003

Yesterday the bombing was further away. I was anxious waiting for the American fighters to come back, but they didn't. At ten o'clock, it was very quiet and calm. What a great thing to live without bombing! Later that night we heard some small explosions.

I spent the morning cooking, washing dishes, and completing some other housework. It's fine though, because it lets me work and forget about the war for a while. After lunch I went to visit our neighbors and we drank some chai together. In the evening, I took another sleeping pill at nine o'clock hoping that it would help me sleep. We had our lunch in the safe room, and I finally fell asleep at ten-thirty.

Then around one in the morning, we woke up to an enormous explosion very nearby, possibly at the airport. The ground was moving as if there was an earthquake, as if something was digging deep in the ground. The explosions continued until the morning. We spent the night trying to take some short naps between one explosion and another.

Faiza Al-Araji

MONDAY, MARCH 24, 2003

My face is pale. I cannot sleep during the night or during the day. We can hear the explosions all day long. They say Americans are bombing the surrounding areas of Baghdad, preparing to enter the city.

Yesterday Iraqi television showed interviews with American prisoners. I don't like to see these things at all. The situation is getting worse. There are battles in the south to invade the Iraqi cities.

We had an electricity blackout for some hours, and its cloudy and cold today. I'm not in the mood to do anything, I feel tired and sleepy; dreaming of the end of this nightmare. When is it going to come?

I have some free time; time that I wish I had in my ordinary life. But it's a depressing, hateful free time now: full of sirens and explosions! I don't like it at all.

Faiza Al-Araji

TUESDAY, MARCH 25, 2003

Last night's bombing was short, but concentrated. Most of it was far from our part of the city.

"Far away," Azzam said, "means it's against the Iraqi army bases."

I feel very sad for those fighting in the Iraqi army; neither new military equipment nor modern military plans are available to them. There is no sense in comparing the capabilities of the two armies: a broken army on one hand, and an extremely high-tech army on the other. I took a long afternoon nap and woke up at around six. The bombing stopped at one in the morning because of the bad weather.

In the silence and darkness of last night, we could hear the noise of the American fighters flying in the sky over Baghdad from time to time, and I wondered, couldn't this military pilot get himself another job? Did he really try to find other alternatives before accepting this evil job? Hiding under the covers, I suddenly realized that this pilot,

5

in the eyes of his countrymen, is a great hero, but from the Iraqi perspective, he is an evil criminal.

Strong winds blew dust around today, but at least there were no explosions. The dust became very dense in the afternoon; the sky was orange and sometimes red and I couldn't breathe because of the concentrated sand in the air. The funny thing is that we couldn't close our windows. If we closed them, a single explosion nearby would break all the glass. We spent the night choking on the sand.

Faiza Al-Araji

WEDNESDAY, MARCH 26, 2003

I got up early in the morning, cleaned the floors, washed the bathrooms, and washed the pathways in the garden. The car park, the garden, and our cars are in terrible condition because of yesterday's dust; in fact, the dust and sand turned out to be mud after last night's rain. Everything is covered with red mud now!

When are we going to get our lives back? When kids will go to school again? When will Azzam and I will go back to our jobs, speak with customers, sell and buy, visit friends and neighbors? When is life going to start again?

Faiza Al-Araji

FRIDAY, MARCH 28, 2003

There was continuous shooting nearby this morning. I was frightened, and I didn't understand what was happening. The anti-aircraft guns were targeting something. Then suddenly people were running in the streets and shouting! What's happening?

Someone shouted, "They shot down a small American plane!"

Raed and Azzam went out to see what happened, and came back with a small part of the downed plane! We kept it as a souvenir.

In the evening, Sho'la market, which is in a dense and poor area, was hit by a missile. There were 55 people killed and about 50 injured. The hospitals were full of injured people, their families, and news reporters. It is such a tragic, painful thing to happen.

Today is a sad day; worse than the previous ones. We are feeling insecure as civilians now. When is all of this going to end?

Faiza Al-Araji

SATURDAY, MARCH 29, 2003

We heard the fighter jets at seven in the morning. There were explosions close by and far away. I was totally terrified, and my nerves were shot. Everything scares me now and I'm shaking all the time.

It's ten in the evening now, and we are enjoying a quiet sky. I spent the evening with Majed, reading some Shakespearean plays.

My heart is really sad because of the casualties of yesterday's bombing at the market. And I'm afraid of what might happen to us while we are in our house. I think everyone thinks every day might be his or her last. We heard a broadcast on the news about a suicide bombing at Najaf.

We put a large map of Iraq in our sitting room so that we can mark where the Americans are day by day; we want to know from which direction they are going to enter Baghdad. I was wondering— what were we going to see first? Tanks? Soldiers? Helicopters?

Faiza Al-Araji

SUNDAY, MARCH 30, 2003

Extremely strong night attacks. Our house was shaking all night. I don't know what they were bombing. In the early morning the glass in our master bedroom was broken. Fortunately, no one was sleeping there. I was very upset. I went with Azzam to clean and collect the glass fragments and we put wood over the broken glass. Our bedroom looks so sad now; first we abandoned it, now the windows are broken.

Every night, after dinner, we go to sleep. Because the whole family is sleeping in the same room now, we spend a long time speaking and laughing in the dark.

At around midnight I heard a siren and started feeling nervous. I hid in the bed and everyone laughed and made jokes about me. I just hate to hear the sound of fighter jets, but Azzam kept on teasing me, "Here they come. Hide." he said and laughed. All I can do is read the Qur'an, and ask God to let the pilot go away without killing us.

I spent the night trying to sleep between explosions, but I just could not sleep. I began to worry about getting some disease because of my constant fear.

At ten in the morning, Abu Selah, the gardener, came to get his salary. We haven't seen him since before the war started. He is a polite, old, poor man with a big family that shares their house with his brother's family. I think they have more than fifteen people living in that house. We invited him to drink chai with us in the kitchen. I asked him, "What are you and your family doing?" He seemed to be sad and depressed.

"Very bad news," he said. There was a moment of silence as we sipped our chai.

"What's wrong, Abu Saleh? What happened?" I asked.

Abu Saleh and his big extended family lives nearby, in a very poor district on the other side of the wide street that divides our neighborhoods. Most of its residents work either as soldiers or as farmers and gardeners. His neighborhood is called the Al-Furat (Euphrates) district. Everyone was expecting that Al-Furat would be a target for bombing, because it is very close to the presidential palace, National Guard center, and airport.

"We left our house," he said. "They attacked the republican guard center last night. Women were screaming and crying. They were shaking like the leaves on a palm tree and they were begging me to take them out of this hell. 'Take us to any other place they said.' "

"Believe it or not Abu Raed, I went out in the middle of the night and brought a truck and put all the girls and women inside it—all of us—the old and the young." Azzam and I were shocked!

"We couldn't even take anything with us, I just asked the soldiers to take care of our house."

"Where did you go?" I asked.

"We hid in a broken down house in Radwaniya."

We felt very bad for what happened to old Abu Saleh.

How can we help you? We were wondering.

He asked us whether we had an extra oil lamp; his family was living in darkness. We gave him one of our two gasoline lamps, and begged him to accept some money, too. "Buy some vegetables for your family," I said. We walked with him to the main door and he promised to come back later this week to let us know what happened to his family. I felt very sad. I thanked God we were still in our home. I wondered how many other families faced the same circumstances. Only God knows, and only He can protect us with His mercy.

Faiza Al-Araji

MONDAY, MARCH 31, 2003

A frustrating morning followed our sleepless night; all I could hear and feel were explosions since sunrise. I tried to go back and sleep a bit at midday, but I had a very painful headache.

Our doorbell rang unexpectedly. A Red Crescent (the Iraqi equivalent of the American Red Cross) car was parked outside our door, and a group of young men and women came out of the car. I remembered them when they entered our guest room. They had come before the war asking for some water purification units for hospitals, and they took some catalogues and price lists at that time. Now they had returned to buy some units. We had some filtration units in our house, hidden under the stairs. We wrote a contract for the sale and drank some coffee. An Italian NGO was with them, Un Ponte Per; they were funding the project. We discussed current events, and criticized Bush and his administration. I don't think he cared for our critique. We are going through this hell alone.

Faiza Al-Araji

TUESDAY, APRIL 1, 2003

I removed the cover from my car and cleaned the dust from it. Raed and Azzam went to take a look at our showrooms and office. It was very quiet outside, so I decided to go for a quick visit and say hello to my sisters and brothers. All the telephone exchange buildings were bombed, and I didn't hear from anyone in the last few days.

First, I went to visit my sister in Saydiya, but she wasn't home. Neighbors said that she is fine, though; she just went out shopping a few minutes ago. Her husband is living abroad, and I feel sad for her situation, living alone with her daughters in these tough days. I felt a bit disappointed; I really wanted to see her.

My next stop was my youngest sister's house. She was with her daughters, and a guard was in the garden. Her husband is a general manager in the Ministry of Health, and she has rarely seen him since the outbreak of the war. He comes back home for several minutes to change his clothes and then goes back to the ministry. Her face was full of red spots. "Because of the stress," she said.

"We sleep in our neighbor's house," she said. "The girls and I are afraid to sleep alone, as the house shakes all night long. The guard is taking care of our house."

I took a look around her house; she had put sheets and covers all over the furniture, just as if it were an abandoned house. I remembered the time all of my sisters used to come and sit here and laugh—that was before the war.

This war is tearing us apart. May God curse every stupid person who participated in starting this war.

I went back home quickly, before the night attacks begin again.

Baghdad looked sad and torn apart; pale with all of that sadness, dust, and black smoke. The condition of Baghdad breaks my heart. I felt that Baghdad was complaining through her silence. Baghdad—my old love—I cried and remembered my mother. Thank God she died and didn't have to see these black days. I didn't like those visits. I wish I didn't leave our home the first time; all I got was more depression and sadness. At night, the bombing was strong, but far away. Sleeping is impossible.

Faiza Al-Araji

WEDNESDAY, APRIL 2, 2003

As Sahhaf holds a press conference everyday. I believe he is either a liar or a moron. The news says the Americans are going to enter Baghdad in 48 hours.

Everyone is on edge. We feel the time is very near. Some people say we shouldn't be afraid, that Saddam is going to let Baghdad be the Americans' graveyard. How? I wonder all the time. We don't even have a single fighter in the sky; the army is without any air cover.

We stay here in our homes, and don't have full details about what's happening out there. But most of the people don't have any real hope. I feel afraid that after this regime falls, other unknown faces will come and obey the Americans' requests.

I don't like them at all, those who are waiting for their new authorities, while we are facing death and fear every minute.

I have great anger and pain inside me because of what is happening. And I feel disgusted of those coming from the outside, reaching their high positions by climbing on the dead bodies of Iraqis who were killed without anyone even noticing.

Faiza Al-Araji

THURSDAY, APRIL 3, 2003

An ordinary, gloomy morning. After lunch, I said to Raed, "Let's go visit your aunt. I want to check if she is safe, for I visited her a few days ago, but didn't find her."

I knocked on her door, but no one answered. The neighbors said she went to Ramadi. A pickup came by and she took some mattresses and pillows, and some of her valuables. My other sister and brother came too, and they all went to Ramadi, where they rented a big house, and planned to return when things calmed down. My heart sank; I felt that something terrible was about to happen. Why did they go to Ramadi? Did they have any knowledge about what was going to happen?

There were no telephones, so I couldn't call and ask for details. But I guessed they had heard some definite news, for my brothers were ex-medical doctors, with a lot of friends, and quite a good supply of reliable news.

Raed said, "Don't be sad, Mom. Let me take you to visit Baghdad. Didn't you ask to go before the war? Come on, this is our chance." I remained silent, having no desire to answer. Baghdad now is battered; what's the use in going there?

The drive took more than an hour. The Sinak communications center was in ruins, as was the Al-Mammon center. Some official buildings and ministries were hit by missiles and the streets nearby had no windows left intact. There was a street in Karrada about which we laughed so much, calling it The Street of Scattered Glass, saying that glass suppliers would make a lot of money after the war.

Baghdad looked like a ghost city: silent streets, devoid of cars and people, with evidence of missile bombardment. That was all I saw on my visit. We arrived back home at around 5 p.m. I was tired, both in body and in spirit.

I wished I could change my clothes and rest for a while. I sat in the safe room, telling Azzam and the boys what we saw on our visit. I was sitting on the floor wearing the same clothes when we heard the artillery bombardment nearby. *What was that?* we all wondered, then asked Raed to go up to the roof and find out what was happening; perhaps the Iraqi defenders set up an artillery position close by.

Raed came running down, panting. There was artillery bombardment from the airport on the Al-Furat District opposite from us. Shells were falling on the streets, people were running. We said, "So the Americans got to the Baghdad Airport," and stared at each other.

We called one of Kahlid's friends who lives in our neighborhood, and asked, "What is happening?"

"An American attack," he said. "We will leave our house now, and you also should leave yours. The area is not safe."

We started hearing shouting and the sirens of ambulances. The sounds of artillery quieted down for a while, but the sirens told us that death was close by. The war was suddenly taking place very close by, with explosions, casualties, and death. I ran upstairs and got a big suitcase, into which we hastily put pajamas for each of us. I felt that I was going to die from panic once more.

Raed said, "Let's wait and see what happens."

But I screamed, "There is no time to think or wait; the American missiles are going to fall on our heads tonight. I won't stay here one more minute!"

Azzam's instructions were for Raed and Khalid to go in one car, and that we were to follow in the other, fearing that if we left the car in the garage it would be stolen. The situation wasn't safe. Where would we go? The nearest relative's house belonged to the boy's uncle, in Saddam District. We decided to spend the night there, a few kilometers away from us to the east, in the opposite direction of the airport.

We drove hastily, in confusion; all the while ambulances rushed past us going in the other direction to the Al-Furat district where Abu-Selah, the gardener, lived. I have never seen so many ambulances before. Al-Furat District was the nearest point to the airport. Perhaps there was an Iraqi military force there; I don't know. But it was a small district, its houses too close and adjacent to each other, the streets narrow.

Raed was driving fast in front of us, and we drove fast to keep up. All the drivers were confused, hurrying in all directions. The streets were full of people leaving their houses on foot; families of men, women, and children carrying small sacks with them, perhaps their clothes and valuables. Some of them waved to the cars begging anyone to carry them far away from here. But there weren't any drivers willing to stop; everyone was trying to get out of this hell as quickly as possible. It was dusk, almost 6 p.m. The electricity went out before we left the house. On the streets you could smell death and smoke and panic. The day of *hell*, that's what I call that day.

Faiza Al-Araji

FRIDAY, APRIL 4, 2003

We spent last night at the boy's uncle's small apartment. We couldn't even sleep, partly from being so nervous because of what happened to us, and partly because of the thundering noises from the Iraqi resistance fire, which bombarded the airport till morning.

At midnight, we listened to the news on the satellite channel; our relatives had a generator. But the electricity was still off, so most of the people didn't know till now. The news said that the American forces tried to land in the airport, and dropped cluster bombs on the Al-Furat district. The Iraqi casualties reached 300 dead, both civilian and military. Al-Sahhaf said, as usual, that it was nothing; we will kick them out and destroy them. I fully realized that he was a liar; that the pit they were leading us into is very, very close. Last night was one of the saddest, fearful, and painful nights—shall we ever go home? I remembered Abu-Selah, who ran away for fear of the bombardment, leaving his house to ruins.

Instead of one disaster, we were facing two: bombs, destruction, panic, and having to leave our house. We didn't even bring any identification papers, passports, or money. We left everything behind and ran.

Just before noon we decided to go home to get more clothes, then go to the Al-Doura area, where the boy's other uncle lives. They had a bigger house, and the area was a bit further away and probably safer. Azzam, Raed, and I went, leaving Khalid and Majed behind; we didn't want the whole family to die in one lot. We found that our area had turned into a ghost town: the streets empty, the houses seemed to be deserted by their occupants. Some soldiers were resting under an umbrella, reclining on the pavement, and talking, with their launchers scattered on the ground nearby. We passed them quickly. I felt my heart twisting in pain for them, saying to myself, *these soldiers are going to die, no doubt*. I stared at the empty streets, looking toward the airport, where a suspicious silence prevailed.

We reached the house to gather some more clothes, and emptied the contents of our safe in a small box. I was very nervous, especially when some shooting erupted nearby. So I said to Azzam, "Let's get out, I want nothing more." The electricity was still off, the refrigerators were starting to thaw, losing their frost. "All the food will perish," Azzam said. I said to myself, *Let it go to hell*.

We closed down the house once more, and I worried if I would ever come back to it. Would I find it safe? I didn't know, so I decided to stop thinking about it, for I already had enough on my mind. We collected Majed and Khalid, then went to Al-Doura in two cars, where we put each one in a separate garage at the neighbors. Most people here were poor, almost no one owned a car, and the garages were empty. We put our luggage in an empty room upstairs. We were sad to leave our house, and embarrassed for being here, for we felt that we would be an added burden to the family, and they would lose their privacy. But this was war, when all privacies are stripped away.

The news says there is a decisive battle going on at the airport; that the Americans have withdrawn to an adjacent area, with fierce fighting raging all the time. All night long the Iraqi ground artillery bombarded the airport, and the American warplanes raided the capital.

It's impossible to sleep.

Faiza Al-Araji

SATURDAY, APRIL 5, 2003

We woke up suddenly, fearfully, of the noises of machine-gun fire, helicopters, and missiles. There was a battle raging outside. We hid in the storeroom, amid rice and flour sacks, and the car's spare parts. The room was small, and there wasn't room for every one, so the women got inside, and the men remained outside; there was unbearable panic. On the main street, coming from the south, the American troops were probably advancing toward Baghdad.

In half an hour or so, the battle ended, and all was quiet. People went out to the street, and came back with news. The American troops had pulled back, and the streets were full of Iraqi corpses. We didn't understand what had happened—and who would tell us?

In the afternoon, Azaam and Raed went back home to get the small generator that we used at the shop. There was no electricity and we wanted to watch the news on TV. Azaam and Raed said that the areas adjacent to the airport were completely evacuated; only vehicles belonging to the Iraqi army, and some soldiers were on the streets. The houses were empty. My heart froze. I felt defeated.

Al-Sahhaf said that the American troops pulled back and we had destroyed them; then he took the journalists to tour the airport road. The T.V. was broadcasting music along with men carrying machine-guns, dancing, and endorsing Saddam Hussein. I was stunned, for I do not usually watch Iraqi T.V. at home. But here I had to; there was no satellite receiver. I was hit in the face by this wretched media, and all those misled people. I had the feeling that these songs would not be broadcasted again; that they had become a part of some past that will never return.

It is evening, and my heart is sad. I remembered the Iraqi soldiers, lying on the pavement, under a canopy of bullets and danger, death approaching, surrounding them. What crime have they committed? Why should they have to pay the price of a foolish man's policy? Deprived of their homes, families, and loved ones—defending Saddam or defending us? We people, sitting home, spending our times as it goes, waiting for this stupid game to end. But these soldiers, they are inside the grinder of death. Silent tears rolled down my face. Unknown soldiers. Who would remember them? I truly wished we could help them defend Baghdad, but how? I didn't know. I felt guilty, powerless to do anything.

Faiza Al-Araji

SUNDAY, APRIL 6, 2003

Another dismal day. Heavy bombardment to the airport area, announcement of a curfew from 6 p.m. till 6 a.m. We ran the generator for a while in the morning as there was no electricity and we were low on fuel. We emptied the refrigerator and the freezer, but so much of the food had spoiled. I felt more depressed as I thought of our house. Is the house still intact; had any shells fallen upon it?

Shall we ever go home, or perhaps be like the Palestinians, who left their houses in 1948, thinking that they would be back within the week, but never returned? Still their grandchildren have the same dream, of returning home. Distant dreams.

The water supply is very weak. We can hardly collect enough water to do the laundry and wash the dishes, and I had washed my hair in the sink. We have some cheap soap, but there was no cream for my hands. I forgot all my personal things at home.

I do miss our life, our home—I feel so lonely.

Faiza Al-Araji

The Iraq War Blog

MONDAY, APRIL 7, 2003

Another morning assault at 7 a.m. The sound of bombardment, machine-gun fire, and warplanes. Heavy dust is cloaking the city. I wondered how our house would fare because we didn't leave the windows tightly shut.

In the afternoon, we heard in the news about a severe missile attack on several houses behind the Al-Sa'aa restaurant. They thought that Saddam Hussein had a staff meeting there; perhaps it was another disastrous hit like the Al-Ameriya shelter raid, with so many civilian casualties. But as we did not leave the house, we hardly knew what was happening. Everybody is hiding in their homes.

Faiza Al-Araji

TUESDAY, APRIL 8, 2003

All is quiet. This was the first night without bombs and planes. I slept since midnight till seven in the morning. What does the world look like without war? Last night I remembered my sisters, friends, and neighbors—where are they? What happened to them? It's as if I am not in Baghdad, as if I have traveled to a place very far away—even though the distances are the same—but we can't contact each other or know if someone is safe.

It is sad the way Saddam and those with him are going to meet their end, but I keep thinking back to all the harmful things he did. He was given many chances to do better, but he never stopped being cruel to the people. He had no compassion for them, never thought of their welfare; only the few he had use of basked in his favors, lived a good life, while most of the people were miserable, and unjustly treated.

And who says his replacement will be better than he was? Only the days to come will show us what is now hidden. And all goes by the will of God Almighty. They say there are battles going on at the Presidential Palace. By evening, we heard about the American bombardment of the Palestine Hotel and the Al-Jazeera office. A number of journalists, reporters, and photographers died.

Another sad day.

Faiza Al-Araji

WEDNESDAY, APRIL 9, 2003

Another morning battle on the road from Yousiffiya to Baghdad, at the Al-Doora intersection—the noises of various weapons—then quiet. The neighbors said there were civilian martyrs killed on the main street, and their cars burned. The American troops had orders to shoot any moving target. People are afraid to collect the bodies of their relatives; the streets are not safe.

At noon, Azzam and I went to find out if there was a way to get back home; the way to the main street was scarred from battle. Cut electricity cables lay in the street, the curbs were broken, and there were holes in the street from helicopter gunfire. Burned Iraqi army vehicles and empty civilian cars, stood by the edge of the road, for here the bodies had been removed. But on the other road, the main road going to the airport—danger—do not get too close. They called it the Death Road; they threatened to kill anyone in the area. So, we went back to our relative's house.

Dust, bombardment, no electricity, imprisonment at home, a curfew, family and relatives leaving town, and a mysterious, unknown future. This sums it all up. At 3 p.m., the American tanks came, then drove into the side streets, and stood on the corner of the market place, the American flag waving, people moving about with their hands raised up or holding white flags; this is how they heard the instructions. There was a skirmish between some Ba'ath party members and the American troops, then all went quiet.

As the tanks moved around in the area, people went into their homes, but kept watching from the windows or on roof tops, cautiously and fearfully. We couldn't understand yet what happened. Where did Saddam Hussein go? We saw him on television yesterday, people carrying him, clapping and praising him, like fools. I think this is the end for him. I remembered the dream I had before the war.

In the evening, we listened to a Monte Carlo radio station announcing that people had gathered in Al-Firdouse square and pulled down the statue of Saddam Hussein. Nobody could believe that! What is happening? How did we get to this? Where is the Iraqi army?

I went up on the roof, then up on the parapet, and gazed at Baghdad far away. The black smoke has stopped; it was sometime after sunset, the sky was clear, the air refreshing. Calmness shrouded the city after the hell of war.

Would the war really stop? Shall we ever get back to our lives again? I wish so, with all my heart.

Faiza Al-Araji

THURSDAY, APRIL 10, 2003

We went back home. The road was accessible from Al-Dora to Al-Saidia. The streets were crowded, a lot of the passengers in the cars held white flags, which they waved from the windows, fearing they would be shot at by the coalition forces. Many people are walking about, carrying a few pieces of luggage, going back home.

The main intersection at Al-Dora, where the coalition forces passed a few days ago, is filled with hundreds of bullet casings and unused bullets, as if they speak of an armed dialogue that took place here.

All the way home there were storage bungalows, official warehouses, and Ba'ath party headquarters. At first, I didn't understand what was happening. Men, women, and children were carrying furniture, fans and coolers, air-conditioners and cookers, carpets and curtains.

Who are these people? What are they doing?

I was confused, but Azzam said, "They are stealing state property." I couldn't believe it!

It was as if there were instructions that gave them a green light to steal. A shameful, degrading sight.

I looked upon them as if they were scum, the same scum that used to run and shamelessly clap for Saddam, "By soul and blood we die for you."

I felt a terrible pain in my heart, a wound deep inside my soul. What is happening?

We reached our house, and the neighbors' son came to us, and said, "Do not be afraid, but you will find all the windows broken and smashed—last night a missile landed on the street and smashed the windows of all the houses—thank God no one died."

We entered the garage, walked toward the wooden main door, which was blown apart from the fierce explosion. Thank God we were not here. I would have died of fear.

We decided to clean the house. Majed and Khalid would gather and sweep the smashed glass, and Azzam would fix the broken door. The sight of our house was depressing, as if it had been abandoned for months. There was dust all over the furniture, shards of broken glass filled the house, and even the pictures had fallen from the walls. Artifacts fell from the shelves onto the floor.

There wasn't a drop of water in the tanks, and no electricity in the house. We turned on the generator, and then pulled the water out of the well that had been dug behind the house, and Raed and I started to clean. We started cleaning at 11 a.m., and finished around 4 p.m. After cleaning, we put large sheets of nylon over the windows, until we could fix new glass for them.

Everyone took a warm bath and put on clean clothes. The weather was starting to get warmer. Then suddenly, there was a powerful explosion behind the house, more windows were broken, the nylon sheets were blown away, and the pictures fell from the walls again. I kept shivering all evening and night. Suddenly, all feeling of safety disappeared.

I kept on reading verses from the Holy Qur'an, so as to calm myself. I cried. I don't know for whom. Myself? The people? The cities? The way we all ended up? Defeated, bitter, and in pain. The news says there is some fighting between Iraqis and Arabs in Al-Mansoor and Al-Adhmiya. And the fear of what is to come—fear of tomorrow—and what it might bring.

A Shiaat leader was assassinated in Najaf. I didn't know him, but they say that America supports him. Well, to hell with that. I hate politics and politicians. I do not understand their language or their interests.

All night long I heard the noises of tanks moving from the airport toward central Baghdad. And explosions in the dead of night. I don't know who is firing on whom. My heart bleeds for Iraq. I cannot even sleep through the night.

Faiza Al-Araji

FRIDAY, APRIL 11, 2003

The garden is full of flowers in many colors, but my heart is sad, and I cannot feel anything toward them.

Will this country ever be safe again? Shall we ever live peacefully? These matters keep worrying me. I do not ever want to leave the country. I want to remain here. I pray to God that all will be calm again; that our lives will go back to normal.

Whenever we discuss the situation as a family, Azzam and I feel optimistic, but Raed says, sadly, "Mother, but it is the occupation, how could everything be all right?" As if he is saying, "Mother, this is a dead man, how can you ask him to speak?"

My heart sinks in sadness; yes, Raed is right. I lose myself in pain and silence. I keep heeding the Holy Qur'an, remembering the verses that threaten the unjust oppressors. I thought of what happened to

Saddam and those around him, how much they humiliated, oppressed, and hurt people.

Now their story is upon every tongue in the world. Their houses were bombed, then robbed. They are scattered on earth; no one knows where they are now. They disappeared, along with all who supported and befriended them, believed in them, and defended them. This is the evidence that God shows to his serfs, so that they would think and consider. Didn't they ever think that such a day would be upon them? Of course not, for the devil was their companion, promising them, tempting them. And God listens, sees, and waits; for they might repent or pray for forgiveness. But their hour came suddenly upon them, and what a shameful end it was: making the wise sad and the enemy gloat. You idiots, what have you done to yourselves?

Satellite channels are transmitting images of the thieves robbing Baghdad, burning the ministries, and looting hospitals. These are not the people, these are the enemies of the people. They will destroy what the bombing has not destroyed in Iraq. Who could love his country, and then do a thing like this?

I remembered something written by a novelist, in which he said that he had visited many cities and found that thieves and prostitutes are the scum of every country; that he couldn't judge that country by these examples because thieves and prostitutes are without patriotism, they do not belong anywhere.

My heart is sad for Baghdad; sad that she is being plundered and robbed of her history and civilization, as if the Mongols have returned, as if the waters of the Tigris are black from the ink of so many books that were thrown in it; books of science and knowledge.

This morning I saw a sad story on TV. The Americans blew up an Iraqi ammunitions storage depot in Utayfiiya that used to belong to the Iraqi Army. The residents gathered, trying to convince the Americans to move the ammunition far away, lest they should harm the people and the houses. But the U.S. Army does not cooperate with the residents; instead the Army blows up the storage building, destroying twenty houses and burning a palm grove. No civilians were hurt because they had evacuated the houses, but they came back to find them in ruins. To whom could they complain? The state has fallen; now there is an occupation, and all rights are lost.

By the end of the night, and after calls for help by the Iraqis through satellite channels, the news says that Bush will give instructions to the leaders of the occupation army to arrange meetings with retired Iraqi police leaders. The priorities are restoring and controlling security, restoring electricity and the water supply, restoring T.V. broadcasting, and restoring public transportation.

In Mosul, Basra, and other Iraqi cities, popular committees were established and leaders chosen for them. These committees fought the thieves and got back the stolen articles. But Baghdad is very big. Who will control security? It is supposed to be divided into smaller sectors, so that the process of establishing the popular committees could start.

They burned some of the ministries: Planning, Irrigation, Commerce, Health, the Property Loan Bank, the Central Bank, and some of the hotels. Who is to benefit from such ugly, harmful acts? Iraq is filled with strangers and enemies, but no honest Iraqi would commit such an act—ever.

Faiza Al-Araji

SATURDAY, APRIL 12, 2003

The chaos is still going on, fires are raging, bank robberies are taking place—even the Iraqi Museum of Antiquities has been looted. People are calling for help through the satellite channels. Who will help us? It is as if the whole world has abandoned us. There is gunfire in the streets; we do not know whether these are thieves or resistance fighters. At noon, some Iraqi policemen appeared on T.V., volunteering to control security in the cities.

Baghdad is sad and gloomy. I am thinking about my brothers and sisters. Where are they? What has become of them? I pray that they return safely to their houses, that God will save them from all harm.

Faiza Al-Araji

SUNDAY, APRIL 13, 2003

Abu-Selah, the gardener came. He and his family are still alive!

Today, there was some news about a meeting at 9 a.m. between the occupation forces and some high-ranking former Iraqi policemen to organize security patrols. We are all waiting for the outcome of this meeting, feeling optimistic about the return of peace to the country. Helicopters have been hovering at low altitude since last evening, perhaps looking for members of the resistance.

Faiza Al-Araji

MONDAY, APRIL 14, 2003

The husband of my neighbor's friend had been missing for ten days. He was last seen in his car and never returned home. Yesterday, they discovered his body on the highway to Karrada, with a bullet in his head. His car was riddled with bullets; he was killed by the coalition forces. Many volunteers removed the bodies from the streets, and notified their kin. My neighbor will visit her daughter and her husband, who were wounded in their house when their neighborhood was bombed by the coalition forces. Apparently, there was a house nearby that belonged to a friend of Uday Hussein.

Why all these mistakes? What have these civilians done? The coalition bombs a house where they *think* Uday is hiding, and many are wounded. The neighbor's son died when the house fell on him; he was only 21 years old. What harm had the poor fellow committed? What is the fault of his parents?

These days we have seen many varieties of torment. First, terrifying air raids day and night. Second, occupation of the residential areas, blowing up tanks and ammunitions depots belonging to the Iraqi army; as a result, houses are demolished and civilians die. Third, the mobs roaming around, the robberies and looting, the fires. All of us are in doubt that these are Iraqis.

The poor Iraqis stole furniture, refrigerators, and coolers. It's possible that they might steal, but they would neither burn the Ministries nor rob the National Museum. These are the acts of organized gangs, who came from abroad, awaiting the chance to strike. People are saying that many mercenaries entered the country with the Americans—mercenaries of many nationalities.

Baghdad is devastated and burned. I wish peace would come back to Baghdad, the homeland of peace. May God have peace upon Iraq and the Iraqis. They say police patrols are about to move about the cities. When will safety return? When will electricity return? When will life return?

Faiza Al-Araji

TUESDAY, APRIL 15, 2003

Azzam and Raed went to my brother's and sister's houses. I feel relieved now; thank God they are all well.

I went with my neighbor to her friend's house to give my condolences for her husband's death. She has three girls and a boy. The girls are young; the eldest of them is only twenty years old and the boy is in primary school. A photograph of her husband hangs in the reception room; he was in his mid-forties, with white hair. He was a merchant. Her voice was sad, her face pale. She told many stories of his warm feelings and affection for his children, and how much he loved to help people. My heart twisted in pain for her and her children, who now have no father. The women in the room told many stories about families who were killed in their cars by random bullets fired by the coalition forces. My grief grew—for people,

Baghdad, and for Iraq. There is a meeting in Nasiriya today between the coalition forces and the opposition party leaders, and there were demonstrations against that meeting.

Faiza Al-Araji

WEDNESDAY, APRIL 16, 2003

I woke up very tired, as if my body and my feelings were crushed.

Yesterday, when I went to the funeral parlor, it was depressing and frustrating. Women wearing black, weeping over a man killed by a stray bullet; talks about neighbors who died last night; talk of the bombing of houses and residential buildings and innocent people killed.

At night I couldn't sleep; the sounds of continuous explosions frightened me, so I ran to another room, far away from the street.

In the morning, Abu-Selah, the Gardener said that the occupation forces were blowing up Iraqi tanks in the Rathwania area.

I feel that this war has devastated my personality and shaken me; that my whole nervous system has become like fragile threads. I feel very weak and exhausted from my grief for people and what has befallen them. For Iraq, for Baghdad—my darling beloved—and what happened to her: Plunder, fire, and destruction. And I tell myself, it all happened by the will of God; there is no God but God, and neither strength nor possibilities unless by the power of God.

And I remembered the Al-Kahaaf verse from the Holy Qur'an, and the dialogue of Moses (God bless him) and Al-Kuther who said to Moses, "How could you be patient about something you know nothing of?"

It is a great disgrace that has befallen us, and everyone makes suggestions and gives speeches, but no one comprehends the truth but God Almighty.

Faiza Al-Araji

THURSDAY, APRIL 17, 2003

I went to Al-Amiriiya and Al-Mansoor. I felt terrible about the shops whose windows were all broken, the houses and multi-story buildings, especially near the Al-Sa'aa restaurant. Our shop was safe, and the shops near it were unharmed. This was the first time I saw it after the war. It was completely empty. When will we go back to work?

I don't know; nothing is clear yet.

Faiza Al-Araji

FRIDAY, APRIL 18, 2003

This was a great day, with masses of worshipers gathered in the mosques, both Sunni and Shiaat.

Dr. Ahmed Al-Kubaisi, the head of the sermon, kindly asked the people to unite and join ranks. He said, "Do not give the occupation the chance to disband you, Sunni, Shiaat, Arab, Kurd, or Ba'athi." After the prayer there was a protest demonstration in which the people said, "Get out of our country before we kick you out."

We all felt happy that day. We felt we are still one nation, one hand, in agreement as to the unity of Iraq, and the necessity of the departure of the occupation. We asked God to keep Iraq and the Iraqis safe, and let this country be peaceful again.

Raed will start working with a non-governmental organization to count the number of wounded and dead Iraqi civilians in all the provinces of Iraq. Majed started to work as a translator with non-governmental organizations. There are no schools, no universities—the young men have a lot of spare time on their hands. They are anxious and willing to participate in something useful.

Faiza Al-Araji

SATURDAY, APRIL 19, 2003

I wish I could work with a humanitarian organization, but the shop will be reopened, and I will be back in my job in about a week, or more, so I could not engage myself with another job.

Khalid went to his college, where they cleaned up their department and organized the library. Many things were stolen and scattered, but they didn't set up a date to resume studying yet.

I went to visit my sister; this was the first time I took out my car. Then, I went shopping in Al-Amiriiya, bought some vegetables and fruit; the prices have doubled three times.

Raed is working with the CIVIC organization; Majed with Voices in the Wilderness; Khalid is still looking for a job.

I wish these days would pass very quickly, and our lives would settle down and go back to normal.

Faiza Al-Araji

MONDAY, APRIL 21, 2003

Azzam and Khalid went to the glass shop near the house. The man came and took measurements of our broken windows, and by evening the new glass was in place. I felt very happy, for the house will remain relatively clean, despite the dust and storms. Without glass, all of the annoying noises reach us very clearly, along with dust and hot air. Of course, I remain afraid of new explosions, and the windows breaking again, but I ask God not to let it happen again. The neighbors also started repairing their windows. All of the prices went up, of course, with the rise in demand, along with the shortage of supply due to the absence of importation or local production.

Faiza Al-Araji

TUESDAY, APRIL 22, 2003

The electricity came on yesterday, and then went off. Perhaps it will take a long time to be fixed and continue to function. The house needs extensive cleaning: the carpets, curtains, and mattresses. I need some help. I went to buy household necessities and the sight of Baghdad is very depressing; it hurt me and broke my heart.

Faiza Al-Araji

WEDNESDAY, APRIL 23, 2003

The sons of Abu-Selah, the gardener came to help me clean the house. We used water from the well because the main water supply is very weak. We washed the carpets, curtains, and mattresses.

I went to my neighbor's in the afternoon for tea. We sat in the garden, then went inside after we heard gunshots from an unknown source.

I shed a tear for Baghdad. I wished I could see a painter, and ask him to paint the following: The destroyed communication centers; the burned-up ministries; the plundered museum; the devastated National Library, which used to be filled with rare, unique scrolls; the universities that were robbed of all documents and furniture; the streets of Baghdad, dirty, filled with garbage and burned cars.

Yes. I shed a tear for Baghdad. It falls on my cheek and the cheeks of all those who love Baghdad.

Faiza Al-Araji

FRIDAY, APRIL 25, 2003

I wish the electricity would come back to the Al-Mansoor area, so the shops could reopen, and we could get back to work. I wish the city were peaceful again, and life would be like it was, so that I could go back to my job. The house cleaning is still going on: we washed the curtains and the cleaned the back garden. We cleaned the dining and guest rooms rugs. I took the plants from inside the rooms to the garden, because they became yellowish, and some parts of them were dead. The rooms now are spotlessly clean, free from the war dust and the sand storms. Today, Tarik Aziz surrendered to the coalition forces and the 55 most wanted American list is now shorter by 13.

Faiza Al-Araji

SUNDAY, APRIL 27, 2003

The cleaning is still going on. We washed the curtains and rugs from the three bedrooms. We rearranged Majed's room as it was before the war. During the war we called it The Fortified Room, and all the family used to sleep there. The weather is dusty; I feel very tired and my whole body is hurting me. I still have to clean the kitchen closets, and the bookcase, the closets in my room and Khalid's. I shall die of boredom.

Faiza Al-Araji

MONDAY, APRIL 28, 2003

I went to my sister's house (she is a pharmacist) in the morning, but I didn't find her. Her daughters told me that she went to open the pharmacy. I was so happy to hear this news. By God's will I too shall go back to work by next week. I bought some things for the house from Al-Amaal Al-Sha'aby Street in Ameriya, where I believe life has begun to come back gradually. In spite of the sporadic electricity, the markets have become more active. Most people buy meat, vegetables, and dairy products every day, because the refrigerators are not working. We are back in the age before electricity.

Khalid, Raed, and Majed went to the Al-Fannar Hotel today, in front of the Palestine Hotel, where they would meet non-governmental organizations, and see some old friends and make new ones. Raed went to Karballa yesterday with Marla from CIVIC Organization, where they started counting the Iraqi civilians

31

wounded and killed during the war. Raed tells painful stories about children who played with cluster bombs, then the bombs exploded, killing them, or filling their bodies with shrapnel. Some had their limbs cut off. Many new casualties enter daily into the southern hospitals; the families of farmers go down the fields to reap wheat or rice, and a cluster bomb explodes from among the plants. Raed said that while he was there, eleven people, members of the same family, were admitted, seven of whom died, and the rest remained seriously wounded. They started printing precautionary posters, warning the citizens of these bombs. I took a few posters to stick in the front window of our shop, and to distribute them to the neighboring shops. Such bombs were dropped upon the Al-Furat District area near our house, the night the coalition forces entered Baghdad Airport, and also upon the Abu-Ghraib area, where casualties occurred when the cluster bombs exploded on people who were cleaning the streets and burning the garbage.

Faiza Al-Araji

SATURDAY, MAY 3, 2003

I started working in the shop. There is no electricity, but the shop is clean and tidy, as Azzam and Abu-Ahmed, our employee, rearranged it, and polished the wooden desk and the bookcase behind it. I was very happy. There is noticeable congestion at the petrol stations. There are unpleasant stories from our customers about killings and car looting, though.

Faiza Al-Araji

MONDAY, MAY 5, AND TUESDAY, MAY 6, 2003

I went to work; there is no electricity again. I saw some unarmed policemen; they disappeared the next day. The Americans are forbidding them to carry weapons; how could they defend themselves or an Iraqi? And now we can't carry weapons to defend ourselves. Who will protect us? The American tanks are roaming the streets, but they are not concerned with the killings or lootings, they do not interfere. What are they doing then? Where is the army? Where is the Iraqi police?

Faiza Al-Araji

MONDAY, MAY 12, 2003

I went back to work; still no electricity. The streets are busy, but there are no police and there is no security. The benzol is being sold on the street corners (black market). There is no cooking gas. The country is in chaos, accidents are increasing every day. I am very depressed.

Faiza Al-Araji

WEDNESDAY, MAY 21, 2003

Electricity is on during the hours of 6 p.m. to 8 p.m., and 2 a.m. to 4 a.m. The Americans are spreading news about achievements they have accomplished, but on the actual ground we see nothing. We don't know whether they are truthful or not.

The schools are open, they are teaching whatever they can; the important thing is that the children finish their school year. Some schools were destroyed during the war, so they merged those students with others from another school, and made the school day into two shifts, morning and afternoon. Then a date for the final exams was fixed, the seventh of June. The universities are in total disarray—with elections—there are some fights between the professors, and among the professors and the students.

This week's slogan is: Eradicate the Ba'ath, launched by Premar. People seem to have gone crazy; they are fighting with each other. They threw down the statue of Ahmed Hassan Al-Baker and the metal statues of the Um Al-Toubol Martyrs were stolen by a gang who then melted them down in order to sell them. And the

Al-Sa'adoon statue, of the Iraqi prime minister during the Monarchic period, was stolen also. His family is complaining and demanding an investigation. All senior Ba'ath officials were dismissed from state offices and from universities and schools. Most professors and teachers were Ba'athis, whether they liked it or not. But no one is listening to their complaints. A state of chaos and aggressive behavior is infecting people.

Faiza Al-Araji

SATURDAY, MAY 31, 2003

Electricity is a little better. Benzol is still a problem, but cooking gas is starting to become available, though expensively priced at 3000 dinars. Before the war, a bottle was sold for 300 dinars. A campaign has begun to collect weapons from the houses. My spirits are better. Azzam is traveling, and I go to work every day. Our business is with private citizens only; there are no state offices or organizations coming to our shop.

Faiza Al-Araji

WEDNESDAY, JUNE 4, 2003

Azzam is in Amman on business. Majed has second-term exams and is busy studying. Khalid goes to the university three days a week. Raed works with the CIVIC Organization to count the dead and wounded. He goes down to the south every Saturday, and gets back on Tuesday or Wednesday night. I worry about him until he comes back as the roads in the south are not safe. There are lootings and killings, too. I keep asking God to keep Raed and those with him safe, as long as they work for the good of the people. Perhaps after collecting the information about the victims they could demand compensation from the American government for the victims' families, for the destroyed houses, or for family members who have been killed or wounded.

I go to work with the driver, and Abu-Ahmed, our employee, who is a neighbor. When I get out of work, I buy fruit, vegetables, bread, and other household necessities, then they drop me at home. I lost a lot of my personal freedom and the joy of driving my car for safety reasons. Most neighbors, relatives, and friends put their valuable cars in their garages, and started driving less expensive cars with a driver.

I took the computer to the shop. Before the war, I used to take a course on computer skills and software, but I seem to have forgotten most of it. I enlisted in the institute for a new, intensive course, and in the afternoon, I arranged with another driver to take me and Khalid to the institute, then take us back home. The streets are forbidding, unsafe, and depressing. There were a few students at the institute; before the war it was full of students. But now that the conditions are a lot less safe, where are the job opportunities? Most state offices are destroyed; the employees stand in the street, or get inside the ministry, only to find no chairs or desks, so they gather daily to meet each other, then go home.

There are many rumors and tales about the salaries; there are worries and hunger in the houses. Some ministries have been disbanded, their employees sit at home, with no past, and no future. The Ministry of Information, the staff of The Radio & T.V., the Ministry of Defense, the officers, the soldiers and their families. Every day there are demonstrations and clashes with the coalition forces; people wonder, what is our fate, and that of our families? I don't know. The general conditions are unclear and depressing.

Faiza Al-Araji

THURSDAY, JUNE 5, 2003

Khaleel, my youngest sister's husband, is a pharmacist. He used to work as a general manager in the Ministry of Health. He had a good reputation in the ministry, and used to help people a lot; now he is meeting with American committees to organize the work of the ministry. The situation is very difficult; there are no salaries for employees and the offices have been burned. The hospitals have also been plundered, but the coalition forces are trying to get the situation under control again. We deem them responsible for whatever catastrophes that took place; there was a delinquency from their side and bad management. Or perhaps they intended these catastrophes to happen. I don't know, but people are angry, asking, "What are thousands of soldiers doing here?"

Khaleel had a brain clot while working at the ministry. They admitted him to the hospital. My sister is in very poor spirits. I went to visit them; he can't walk or talk. I felt very sad for him. He is only in his early forties and facing lots of pressure. His wife said he will die of sorrow for what happened to the ministry, and she shall be widowed, and her daughters left without a father. She had a fight with him, telling him to leave his job, for he will either die of exhaustion, or some malicious idiot will assassinate him. Perhaps he will travel abroad for treatment.

Gangs are still killing and looting. Many families still have missing family members, whom they are looking for. Most of them went missing during the entry of the coalition forces into Baghdad. The roads were closed, so nobody heard any news. Perhaps they died during the fighting between the coalition forces and the Iraqis. People mostly are divided into two factions: some support the Americans and feel optimistic about their presence, while others do not see good in their presence. Some resistance operations have started, and missiles were launched at the Americans. We say it is still too early to judge them; give them a chance, and we will see the truth with time. We will know if they were truthful or lying.

Faiza Al-Araji

MONDAY, JUNE 7, 2003

The electrical engineer who was repairing my car a week ago, then disappeared, came back to my shop. His head and hand were bandaged, and there were scars on his face. He apologized for the delay, as an armed gang attacked him, attempted to steal the car of a customer he was driving with. But the owner refused to give up his car keys; he activated the alarm system, crippling the car, and threw the keys away. They beat the owner until he passed out, then left him in the street; this happened in broad daylight. Then they tied the engineer's hands, blindfolded him, and put him the trunk of the car. They took him to a house in a crowded, popular area, Al-Washash, were there weren't any Iraqi police or American soldiers. They beat him in punishment for not helping them get the keys. In the afternoon, an old man came by, perhaps the captor's father or uncle. The engineer begged him to let him go free and return to his family in Mosul because he was blameless in the matter, as it was the owner who refused to give up his car. The man felt sorry for him, gave him a clean shirt to replace the bloodied one. They covered his eyes, then dropped him off on the main street, where he spent the night at a relative's house. He came to see me to say good-bye and he went home. I felt badly for him; the story bothered me very much. I decided not to use my car from then on. I arranged with my neighbor's son, who had recently lost his job with the state to take me to work every day, then take me back home at noon.

Faiza Al-Araji

SUNDAY, JUNE 8, 2003

I started my typing and computer course. My mood isn't what it used to be; in former courses I was more cheerful, but today I find myself frustrated, with no desire at all to learn anything. I don't know, maybe war changes people for the worst. The city has some new newspapers. Majed works with the Al-Muwajaha (Confrontation) Newspaper, which criticizes the coalition forces. The coalition forces sent someone to the press office asking about the paper and its writers. I am afraid they might take Majed to prison.

I said to him, "Darling, we don't want any trouble. We just got rid of Saddam. Perhaps they have democracy in America, but I do not suppose they will treat us as they would treat their people; for us they are occupation forces."

Majed said, "I wish they would arrest one of us so we could expose them. Where is the democracy?"

"Oh, my son, why do you love trouble?"

He laughs and says, "Mama, don't be a coward, let us walk a new path."

I believe he is right, but I fear for him. I do not want him to get hurt. Yet, I don't want to deprive him of experiencing life. Our generation was wronged; yes, we studied, learned, worked, and were successful, but we were deprived of the opportunity of making better lives for ourselves. Perhaps this is a chance to begin our lives anew. I would love for Majed and his generation to have their freedom, and succeed in making a better future for their generation. I like their daring and enthusiasm. I pray that God keeps them safe. They go out every day with cameras and interview people, sometimes interviewing soldiers from the coalition forces, who are ordered not to speak with anyone. We hope they go back to America and tell their government to pull its troops from Iraq, but I do not think they could do such a thing. Most of them come from poor families and need the salary. Why should they be concerned with Iraqi misery?

Faiza Al-Araji

MONDAY, JUNE 9, 2003

A customer came to the shop with some materials used in water purifying systems. I knew these materials were not imported individually, because they were missing from the market before the war, and only state organizations had them. He brought samples, and asked me if I would buy from him.

I asked him first, "Where did you get them? Confess," I said, laughing.

"Do you want the truth?" he asked, naively.

"Yes, tell me the truth," I said, in a loud voice. There were other customers in the shop, and I wanted others to hear our conversation. He said he stole them from state organizations. Why? He said that Saddam Hussein executed his uncle, who was in the army.

"And did your uncle come back alive? Or is he happy in paradise?" I asked him.

"How should I know?" he said. His shoulders shook. "Then what should I have done?"

I felt angry, because of his stupidity, and the crime that he doesn't realize he has committed. My laughter turned to anger, and I said, "And what should I tell my maker on judgment day? That I bought stolen materials from you? As if I have shared your sin."

He left, dragging his feet, completely let down, then returned, begging once more, "Okay, give me a piece of advice, for a Muslim brother."

I wanted to roar in laughter, but the situation was serious. I shouted angrily at him, "And what have you left to Islam?" I wanted to get up and slap him in the face, hoping he would realize what he was doing. I thought about him for the rest of the day, remembering our conversation, but then my blood would start boiling in anger. I kept grumbling about him and his foolishness. The customers and employees in the shop were laughing, telling me not to mind him, that he is scum. I was very sad, because this behavior was new to us; this ignorant thief is an enemy of his country, and he doesn't know it.

The government officials are fighting among themselves, Ba'athis and non-Ba'athis, top officials and minor officials. People on the streets are divided. No police, no army, no state; only a coalition force roaming the streets in tanks, not believing they are really here, living in a world that is not connected to ours. We are all wondering why they came, what are they doing? No one knows the answer; maybe in time we shall find out.

Faiza Al-Araji

TUESDAY, JUNE 10, 2003

The connections are back with some of the communication centers, so I was able to call my sisters, and I felt reassured about their safety.

Our affairs changed very much from what they used to be before the war. Now we always make sure we are back home before the sunset prayer call; that is, before it gets dark, because the killings and thieving increase with darkness. At sunset we close the main gate, and when the bell rings, Raed goes out to the garden, carrying a Kalashnikov, with Azzam, Khalid, and Majed behind him.

The visitor would turn out to be one of the neighbors, or someone whose car had run out of petrol, so we take pity upon them and help them. We end up laughing, mocking the irony of the way we look, as if we were living in a jungle without security. The feelings of security and trust have left us, and no one knows from where calamity might strike.

I look at the Al-Muwajaha Newspaper, which is edited by a group of young men, Majed among them. It carries various articles. There is an article about the Society of Free Prisoners, which is trying to locate missing political prisoners, and there is a continuous search for mass graves, the secret tunnels, and underground prisons.

Another article talks about some Palestinian families who were thrown out of their houses, and are now living in tents in a sports club, while the Iraqi Red Crescent is trying to help them. There are about 240 families. I do not know the reason for such frantic hostility, for these are not the Iraqi manners. Some of these families traveled to Jordan, as they had Jordanian passports, but no one received those who had Palestinian-Iraqi traveling documents. I don't know what crimes these people committed; there is some ambiguity in this story.

In another article in the newspaper, there is a part of an interview by the American press with Donald Rumsfeld in Washington, D.C., as he comments on what is happening in Iraq, Rumsfeld said that freedom is chaotic, and people are free to commit crimes and do bad things. I don't understand how these people think!

Do they live like this in America? People killing, looting, and committing all sins. Is this really *The Freedom*?

There is also an article about a theatre group of young Iraqi men and women, who entered the Al-Rashid Theatre, which was destroyed by the bombing, and among the debris, performed a spontaneous play called, *They Passed Through Here* (meaning the forces of invasion and destruction). The audience consisted of some journalists and the friends and relatives of the actors. The actors wondered, *What exactly is freedom?*

The play said that Iraq survived the war, but the war is not over yet. What is over is only one face of it, the face of bombs and missiles. Now it is time for the war of the spirit, and as the winner in the bombs war is the more technologically advanced, so the winner of the spirit war shall be the most loving.

Still there was one more article, which frightened me the most, and I didn't believe it. I felt afraid for Majed because of it; because he was the one who conducted the interviews with a group of Jordanian and Palestinian University students who study in Iraqi Universities. Their houses were raided, they were detained, some of them in their nightclothes, and were taken to the prisoners of war detention camp in Um-Qaser. Some of them were released after two weeks of insults and questions like, "Where is Saddam Hussein?" or, "Describe yourself to us." Then they would laugh at them.

I could not believe—but Majed swears they are truthful—that they said they would leave Iraq immediately, abandoning their studies, while the rest of their colleagues are still detained, their fate unknown. Some of them were students who are members of old Palestinian organizations, like Fatah or the Public Front. Who exposed them, and where did the lists of their names and addresses come from? A very fishy story, and one that raises suspicions. What is the benefit to the American army in all these matters? Or perhaps the Mossad are here, and these are their duties. I don't know, anything is possible, but I am certain that we shall soon find out.

Most of the newspapers issued after the war applaud the occupation forces, publish news about following Saddam and his aides, and bin Laden; about huge projects that will soon return life back to the Iraqis, and we are all waiting impatiently for the rebuilding of Iraq.

Faiza Al-Araji

THURSDAY, JUNE 12, 2003

Strong explosions at the Airport Street at 4 p.m., then again at 10 p.m. The daily comments of people are, "What is the use of these explosions? And if American soldiers are killed in it, that will not change the policy of the American administration to pull out their troops."Even if half of the American army was killed here, they will send replacements. So, it is worth their sacrifices for the sake of their interests, but what shall we gain?Nothing but pain, chaos, and the lack of security. I don't know. I find myself frustrated, and at a loss as to what is happening.

Faiza Al-Araji

FRIDAY, JUNE 13, 2003 - MONDAY, JUNE 30, 2003

Various events.

First, a new car arrived, a Mercedes that Azzam bought from the U.A.E. Baghdad is teeming with new cars, all models and brands. As a result, traffic jams are increasing in Baghdad.

We received new merchandise for the shop for the first time since the war began, but the expenses of transportation and insurance are so high that we will be forced to raise the prices of filters and other items.

The generator burned up, and we bought a new one, a bigger one, to endure working most of the daily hours, as there seems to be no apparent improvement in keeping electricity flowing.

An unbelievable thing occurred recently; it defied explanation. We had an engineer working in the shop with us as a partner since we opened. He is a Christian; he is very polite and honest. He took care of a lot of the administrative transactions, so we gave him a lot of authority to make his job easier. The shop rent contract was in his name, so was the membership card for the Iraqi Chamber of Commerce and the Importation License. There was much trust between us; he received a high salary and a yearly percentage of sales profits.

We saw nothing of him after the war. We assumed that because the streets were closed and the phone lines were down that he couldn't get in touch with us. He sent a letter two days ago by messenger, saying he wanted the shops, for they belonged to him, and he was threatening to use legal methods if we did not negotiate with him. We found this surreal. There was no written agreement between us saying this property belonged to us, so he could rob us and destroy the whole family. We were bewildered, for this was the last thing we expected. This war reveals the vileness in some people's souls.

What is happening in the world? I don't get it.

Faiza Al-Araji

TUESDAY, JULY 1 - SATURDAY, JULY 5, 2003

We had negotiations with the engineer (Nabeel) today to solve the problem. I think Raed had a major role in the matter. Raed always respected him, and used to call him Uncle Nabeel. We visited him often in his house; my sons loved his sons, played with them, and pampered them, because they are much younger than our boys. After that silly message, Raed was so angry, and felt sad because of this shameful conduct; then, by chance, he met Nabeel at a friend's house. Raed shouted in his face, "If you wouldn't give up the contracts, I shall come to your house with my friends, and show you how to reconsider, and I want to come to an understanding with you in front of your wife and children."

It seemed that those words frightened him, and made him give up. Azzam and I refused the idea of threatening him, because we don't want to be scum, like him, but Raed's method worked. The man came begging, asked for some money, resigned, and then withdrew from our lives. But the blow was severe to us. Trust in others makes people happy, and gives reassurance, but today we feel a great bitterness, and fear of what will happen latter. We have to look for another engineer to help us in the shop. Where shall we find him in these harsh conditions when there is no more trust between people?

Faiza Al-Araji

MONDAY, JULY 7, 2003

In the morning, we were surprised to find the locks of the shop broken. There was an unsuccessful attempt to break into the shop last night. I was very annoyed; nothing like this happened since we opened in 1998. I remained tense all morning and sent someone to buy me new locks. I felt things were getting much worse with the lack of security, and the absence of a state, the police force, and an army.

Faiza Al-Araji

TUESDAY, JULY 8, 2003

At about 11 a.m. a relative of Azzam's came to the shop to ask for him. Apparently, he had quarreled with the owner of the building about the new rents; the owner had asked him to evacuate the building. I didn't exactly understand what happened, but I saw the building owner come into the shop, and start beating Azzam's relative, so the other employees pushed him outside the shop into the street. I saw him get mad; he carried a wooden chair and started smashing all the shop windows. The shelves fell to the floor, the filters on them were broken, and I heard the curses and filthy words, "You are

Palestinians, curse your fathers, and curse Saddam who brought you to Iraq!" Oh, my God, this was the first time ever I heard such malicious talk from an Iraqi against an Arab living in Iraq.

I watched the whole act, never moving from my seat. I thought to myself, he might hit me, or call me names, so I preferred to remain silent. I called by intercom, between the shop and our office where Azzam works, and told him quietly, to come to the shop quickly. I told him I had a problem, a man who attacked us and broke the front window. In a few moments Azzam arrived. The sight of the shop was amazing, as if a hurricane had passed through. The goods were upside down, and things were broken; everything was clean and tidy just a few minutes before.

Azzam went out and returned shortly with a few Humvees and some American soldiers. They looked around, asked a few questions, and then apologized that this wasn't their concern. They said, "There is a new police station at Yarmouk, go and file a complaint there," and then they left, so Azzam went to the police station to file the complaint. I used to tell them, "This is the heritage that Saddam Hussein left for us, but today I do not think that Saddam Hussein alone was the reason. This war, the fall of the state, the absence of authority, all these revealed out the hidden, ugly faces of some people—faces full of evil and hatred to others and probably to themselves.

Azzam came back with an Iraqi police car. I rose up from my seat, and stood looking at them walking on the sidewalk. They had brought the aggressor, his head bowed, and his hands behind his back. I told him, "You do not have the dignity of men; you are a man without honor. Didn't you feel ashamed? Didn't you say this is my neighbor, a woman? How did you allow yourself to enter my shop and smash it like a raging bull? Where did you learn these manners?" I wanted to spit in his face, but my manners wouldn't let me. The police car took him away, where he signed an apology paper, and vowed to repair the damages at his cost.

Faiza Al-Araji

WEDNESDAY, JULY 9 - FRIDAY, JULY 11, 2003

I didn't go to work today. Feeling the loss of security is a fearful thing. What is happening to us? Chaos is raking our lives, shattering our unity. We have become like strangers, each afraid of the other's betrayal.

Faiza Al-Araji

SUNDAY, JULY 13, 2003

The first meeting of the Governing Council.

People are divided. Some are optimistic, hoping that these people are the core to establishing a new Iraqi state, but others consider them not worthy to be Premier or the civil Governor. I don't know which of us is right. The coming days will show us more.

Faiza Al-Araji

THURSDAY, JULY 17, 2003

We employed a new person. Today he informed me that his car was stolen from his garage yesterday. Inside the car were ten water-purifying systems for hospitals. An unconvincing story; suspicions point to the new employee, but we have no evidence. What is happening to us? Mishaps never seem to stop, as if a curse has struck us all.

Faiza Al-Araji

TUESDAY, JULY 22, 2003

An historic day: A house in Mosul was bombed. In it were Uday and Qusay, the sons of Saddam, and Qusay's son. All three were killed.

Faiza Al-Araji

WEDNESDAY, JULY 23, AND THURSDAY, JULY 24, 2003

Pictures of Uday and Qusay are all over the newspapers. I can't believe it; no one does. What a terrible end. They say every one's end resembles his own life; yes, their end was cruel and ugly, like their lives. Who shall learn the lesson? I see people like fools, beating each other, not caring for the lessons before their eyes.

Faiza Al-Araji

FRIDAY, JULY 25, 2003

Azzam came home from Amman. He said his car was stopped by an armed group, and they stole his wallet, watch, and wedding ring. We were shocked. What is happening to us? No one has an explanation. The occupation forces are filling the streets, but they are useless. Why are they here? What are they doing?

Faiza Al-Araji

SUNDAY, JULY 27, 2003

Dr. Muhammad Al-Rawii was assassinated in his clinic in front of his wife and patients.

What insolence, what a waste to Iraq. He was an intelligent, brilliant mind, and a leading doctor. He was chairman of the Doctor's Union, the head Dean of Baghdad University, and before all that; he was a close friend of my three brothers, all doctors. My late mother, God bless her soul, loved him, and treated him like one of her own boys.

My heart was wrung in sadness for him, his wife, and three boys. I couldn't go to the funeral, but all my brothers and sisters went. I don't know—I preferred to stay away, and be content with my sadness, without seeing his wife and children, for that would have increased my pain, and I can handle no more.

I went to console my brother, for he was his childhood friend. I found him extremely upset. I cried, feeling the weakness and injustice, but all of us are helpless. There are some new, unknown enemies surrounding us, destroying our lives, while we stand in disbelief.

Faiza Al-Araji

FRIDAY, AUGUST 1, 2003

Khalid finished his University exams, and went to work with an Italian, non-governmental organization (NGO), A Bridge To, with Simona Torrita. We all love her, and treat her like one of the family. Raed works with the CIVIC organization, doing a count of dead and wounded Iraqi civilians; they have almost finished the task, and he is preparing to establish an Iraqi NGO, I'IMAR (Renovation), to rebuild the Iraqi civic society in Baghdad and the southern provinces.

Majed works at the Al-Muwajahaa Newspaper and with Raed. Azzam is always busy working and traveling. And I hide at home after work, reading the Holy Qur'an, and other books, away from the world, the people, and the news of daily disasters.

Faiza Al-Araji

SATURDAY, AUGUST 2, 2003

Uday, Qusay, and Qusay's son, Mustapha, were buried in Tikrit. The sight was painful, but these are the ways of the world. Who learns?

Faiza Al-Araji

THURSDAY, AUGUST 7, 2003

The Jordanian Embassy was bombed today. The dead and wounded were Iraqi civilians. Who benefits from such criminal acts?

My youngest sister and her daughters traveled to Amman, fearful of threats. Her husband is in Amman; he went for medical treatment, but didn't come back.

I was saddened by the separation, but her safety is more important. I will have to be patient.

Faiza Al-Araji

TUESDAY, AUGUST 19, 2003

The Al-Qanat Hotel, the United Nations Headquarters, was bombed today. What is happening to us? Where did those criminals come from? Iraq has become a killing field. And we are dreaming of building a new country. What is happening here? Who is tearing apart our dreams?

Faiza Al-Araji

THURSDAY, AUGUST 21, 2003

I sit at home after I get back from work—lonely, afraid, and depressed. I have a feeling that the joyful times are over. When Saddam Hussein fell, we thought that evil was eliminated from the world, but today we see greater evils.

What is happening? Where are we going?

Faiza Al-Araji

FRIDAY, AUGUST 29, 2003

The bombing of a car in Najaf and the killing of Ayyatullah Baqir Al-Hakeem, the Shia'at leader; hundreds of Iraqis dead and wounded.

Oh, my God. Our lives are turning into a nightmare.

Faiza Al-Araji

SEPTEMBER, 2003

We went to Amman. Raed, Salam, and Simona in one car. Khalid, Majed, and I in another.

Amman: quietness, security, and another world. But it's a world in which I smell danger and estrangement. I miss Baghdad and cannot forget her.

The boys go out with their friends and I remain in the apartment, sitting in a chair on the glass balcony, staring at the city streets and buildings, day and evening.

How lovely is the security and quiet. I wish the same for Iraq and the people of Iraq.

I do feel a deep foreboding and miss Baghdad.

Faiza Al-Araji

OCTOBER, 2003

Raed is working with the I'IMAR organization. Khalid and Majed are at school and University.

The rhythm of life is worrying, scary, and gloomy; security dwindles day by day. Constant explosions and assassinations. The Governing Council has no authority to improve the conditions.

The coalition forces roam the streets night and day, but no improvements come to our lives. Things are becoming worse and only God knows where we are heading.

Faiza Al-Araji

FRIDAY, NOVEMBER 21, 2003

You cannot imagine the scene at Nasiriya. Houses within a radius of 1000 meters of the explosion have no windows, no doors, and cracks in their walls. The explosion was so huge that it blew the doors off the neighbors' houses and knocked down fences and tore up trees.

Two men were crossing a bridge in a car and the passenger started shooting and killed some Italian guards. The car went directly into the main door of the building and exploded, killing everyone in the street and most of the Italians. The heads of Italian soldiers were found hundreds of meters away from the explosion. Some Iraqis were burned in their cars in the middle of the street.

The looting started five minutes later; all the machine guns and pistols disappeared in minutes. Now you can get an Italian pistol for $250 in the gun markets of Nasiriya. Abbas, a restaurant owner, saw some people steal a ring from the finger of one of the dead Italians. The looting continued the next day; this time, furniture and air conditioning units were taken. The strange thing is that everyone at Nasiriya was expecting the attack two days before it happened. Even the policemen and people from the political parties (controlling the city) were going around the streets searching for the car bomb, that's why when the explosion happened people started demonstrating against the police and parties accusing them of not doing their job; upset that they are spending their money on meetings and checkpoints.

Raed Jarrar

TUESDAY, NOVEMBER 25, 2003

I am angry now. "They" come and ask you "why don't you like us?" I will tell you why. I was just stopped at an American checkpoint. They made me stand in the rain and mud for more than 15 minutes. A soldier pushed me so roughly that I nearly fell down, and the other was interrogating me.

"Why do you have a camera in your car?" What the hell! I have a camera? Why not? Then the other American asked me with a smile, "Do you film porn?"

I heard that but I asked him, "What sir? and he replied, "Porn," and then spelled it. Isn't this funny? Soldiers stopping people during Eid (these are the Muslims' festival days), asking them whether they

51

film porn and pushing them into the mud. Soldiers are not the best representatives of any culture.

Raed Jarrar

MONDAY, DECEMBER 1, 2003

We had neither electricity nor matches last night, and we kept calling Abo Hussein, the guard, to lend us his lighter every couple of hours. This problem with services is really strange; even other basic stuff here, like petrol and other oil derivatives are not easy to find. Cars either wait in long lines for hours to get some petrol, or they will buy some from the "black" market. Besides the chance that you get to socialize while waiting, it's not worth spending hours of your life pushing your car (because no one leaves his car's engine on for all of that time), and waiting for a thief to rob you or something. Or maybe it's just our new government's plan for building bridges between the different ethnic groups of the Iraqi people.

What the hell does "Support Democracy in Iraq" mean? You know what I'm talking about, the small logo on your left hand. Who is exactly is the one who is supposed to support Iraqi democracy?

Raed Jarrar

TUESDAY, DECEMBER 2, 2003

Why are camels always related to Arabs in the Western media? It's just like me having an image in my mind about Canadians and penguins. Hey, are you really Canadian? Cool! Do you have a penguin in your bedroom? Do you eat them?

The media. It can easily put images and ideas in anyone's head. It's like the endless crisis of searching for the "truth." Isn't everything just relative? You have two people coming back from Samara, one telling you about the bloodshed that happened: "Dozens of civilians were killed there!" The other with his version of the story: "Nah, nothing happened. It was the usual "ambush" and soldiers freaked out and shot eight people; two were Iranian tourists." Go to the *BBC* and the *CNN* Web sites and you will find the first story; go to *Al Jazeera's* Web site and you'll read the second. They sound like two parallel universes!

At the time of Al Kindi it was a bit easier to speak about truth. He said, "We should not be ashamed to acknowledge truth from whatever source it comes to us, even if it is brought to us by former generations and foreign peoples. For him who seeks the truth there is nothing of higher value than truth itself." Maybe life was better before everyone started listening to the news.

Raed Jarrar

TUESDAY, DECEMBER 9, 2003

I have decided to share the secrets with you. From this place in Baghdad, my sad beloved Baghdad, to tell you the secrets.

Khalid Jarrar

SATURDAY, DECEMBER 20, 2003

The most important streets in Baghdad are closed for security reasons. and people have to wait for up to 12 hours just to get their limit of 30 liters of petrol. One can buy it from the black market for 20 times the price, but one also risks being caught and facing 10 years in prison. Did I forget to thank the Americans for liberating us? How rude of me!

Khalid Jarrar

MONDAY, DECEMBER 22, 2003

It's five in the evening. The electricity just came back on; it has been off since five in the morning. I always wonder how families who do not own an electricity generator manage to wash their clothes or heat their homes since the alternatives are so scarce. Kerosene and cooking gas are almost totally unavailable on the market, and if you do find them they are expensive. And when it comes to gasoline, the lines in front of gas stations are so long they go on for kilometers.

Before the war we were under sanctions for years and we slowly got used to the situation: How to survive and manage in our reality. And although we were cut off from the rest of the world (no satellite TV, no communications and no Internet), we were happier than we are now. I do not know exactly why, but we were like a family living its troubles and secrets, the good ones and the bad ones, in a house that had closed doors and windows. The people abroad would wonder about us; some liked us, some hated us, but we didn't care much because like many other people each one of us was living his life with its infinite details and sorrows, with ambitions for a better tomorrow.

And today the doors have been pulled open, noise and chaos rule the house, and the people who live in it are killing each other, stealing from each other, and hurting each other. I ask myself, *where did all this hate hide for so long?*

And then a lot of strangers came; some wanted to help but many more wanted to harm us for their own reasons. It doesn't matter, the result is the same.

How do I start my day? A driver comes to drive me to work since I am not allowed to drive my own car; it has been in the garage for almost six months because of all the incidents.

On my way to work we take the airport highway; all the trees have been cut down so there is nowhere for anyone to hide who might attack the American forces. The road is deserted now. Then suddenly speeding convoys of Humvees go by. The end of the convoy is an open car with American soldiers pointing their rifles at our cars. I tell the driver to slow down and to try to stay away from them as best he can, so that we do not become the victims of a stray bullet from the gun of a soldier who came to liberate Iraq.

Faiza Al-Araji

It is funny what happened here in Iraq. One day you see people and they all seem to love Saddam; they seem to be happy with the system and the Ba'ath party, and most of them were actually attending the party meetings.

The next day at the university, after the war began, I saw the same people I have seen for the last four years—the same faces—but now they all have different opinions! Some of them turned out to be Saddam haters; others still love Saddam and defend him. A doctor who used to lead the Ba'ath party meetings is now giving us lectures about how happy we should be for getting rid of Saddam!

Saddam is one of the very few individuals on the planet that I hate. But still, I was not happy to see him in "their" hands. I am sorry to disappoint you CIA folks, but I didn't receive your soldiers with roses and I wasn't happy about Saddam's arrest. Know why? Although we hated him, although he destroyed our lives, our economy, and even our religion, he was still one of the few left who weren't involved with the American conspiracy. I mean he was one of the few who said NO to the devil (American fellows—nothing personal—it's your government I am talking about). The bad guys won.

I like American people. I like all people. We all are human beings, we all have the same dreams, we all have the same hopes, we all have the same ambitions; we laugh, we cry, we want to raise our kids in a safe environment; we want peace, we want to feel happy, we want to love and be loved. Isn't that right? We had a simple life, one in which life's basic needs were cheaply available, where security was not an issue. We used to drive home at 3 a.m. and feel safe. Although our society did not allow us to speak out about politics, and people were killed for cursing Saddam, at least we could leave our homes without worrying about being insulted by American soldiers at checkpoints. Now we are afraid the soldiers will suddenly break into our homes looking for someone or something and destroy and steal everything in the process. I am afraid to criticize the Americans. Because Paul

Bremer actually enacted a law in which anything said against the occupation is considered to be an attack.

Khalid Jarrar

TUESDAY, DECEMBER 23, 2003

Last week I went to Sulaymania, a city in northern Iraq, for a short business trip. The people there are good Kurds who respect their visitors. During the visit, as part of our agenda, we had to meet with the local leader of a Kurdish party. He was very friendly, but during my conversation, I mentioned the term "Northern Region." He interjected and said, "Don't use that term please."

I didn't understand what I had said that angered him. He continued, "You are an Arab female from Baghdad and you are not aware that we (the Kurds) wish for our area to be called Kurdistan; we want a federal system and you guys in Baghdad won't agree!"

I realized that I had opened up a wound that these people have been suffering from for a long time. I was accused of being a racist who has no concern for their dreams. I returned to the hotel and was upset for the rest of the day. Yes there is a long history of repression and injustice carried out against the Kurds by the Arabs, but I am innocent of that and I do not support such treatment. But still, each side is united against the other.

Before our return to Baghdad, they took us to visit some buildings that used to house the security apparatus. We saw many squares, gardens, and the stairs leading onto dark corridors where the interrogation and torture chambers were. As I walked through the place I couldn't help thinking, *who can save one human being from another human's injustice?* Even the humanitarian agencies have failed to aid the weak and oppressed.

It is cold and rainy today. Rain is a beautiful gift from the Lord. But when I was little I used to hate rain; it would mess up my hair and I would feel angry and frustrated. But now I see it has many other meanings; it irrigates the land, it tells people of good things coming to them, and washes the roads and trees. How I wish it could wash away the evil from people's hearts.

During the war, Iraqi TV showed pictures of the American POWs and many of us saw in this a very inappropriate and inhumane act. These prisoners looked sad and were shaking in fear; they were so far away from their country, families, and government.

The general situation here is frustrating. There are no new projects to give work to the jobless, no visible reconstruction movement encouraging people to contribute and giving them hope. After all the pain and sorrow they have seen during and after the war, the only issue we hear about is the constant running after enemies, fictitious and real.

And there is no electricity, no gasoline, no cooking gas, or any sort of oil product. If we are such an oil-rich country, where is the oil? Of course you read and hear all sorts of official statements, but all of them are not convincing. The people get bored and nothing is changing for them, they still stand in lines. Things are difficult to get and the promise of a beautiful future is still far away.

I woke up at half past six in the morning. Made breakfast and woke up the kids and we had breakfast together. Khalid went to his university and Majed went to school.

It is still very cold here, and at half past seven the electricity went off. I turned on the generator and sat for a short while reading yesterday's papers, then I flipped through the satellite channels to watch the news. Then I went back to the kitchen around eight and prepared today's lunch for the family (soup and a pasta casserole).

The driver was late and he apologized saying that the traffic jams in front of the gas stations were blocking the streets. In the store where I work, a lot of customers came in; many of them were edgy. I was a bit tense because the electricity kept going off when I was online trying to find articles about water pollution and purification. I have achieved nothing of what I had planned to do today.

I was born in Baghdad and lived here for a long time. I left Baghdad in 1976 after I graduated from college, got married, and came back to her after the first Gulf war in 1991 with my husband and three kids. I never became part of any political movement or party, because I believe that when you become a member of a political party you become a slave to that party, and you don't make your own decisions anymore.

When I returned to Baghdad I found that people, young and old, men and women had become Ba'athists, willingly or not. I didn't like Saddam. I was never one of his supporters. When the "happy" occasions would come, like Mr. President's birthday, and those heroic young men came knocking on the shop's door asking us to contribute to an ad in the newspaper congratulating the president on his birthday, or asking for money as a contribution to the celebrations, they know it is blackmail, nothing else, but who is to say no? And the newspapers are filled with hypocritical poems of love and praise for Mr. President our leader.

Today, there are more than 100 newspapers in Iraq; some are party mouthpieces and some are independent. In some of these papers the staff is made up of former journalists who used to cheer, applaud, lie, and give lip service to survive; now they do the same but they curse, make fun of, and use bad language to describe the former Mr. president, our leader, who is now the cowardly dictator. Why are they doing this? To live? Or to release years of buried hate?

I am confused. Have these people been corrupted by Saddam or were they always like this and there is no way to deal with them? I am depressed and have a headache.

Faiza Al-Araji

WEDNESDAY, DECEMBER 24, 2003

I woke up seven in the morning, a bit later that usual. The house was dark and cold. I don't know why this description reminds me of a grave. We had a quick breakfast and then the kids went out to their studies. Azzam and Raed are sleeping. I am happy when Raed spends the night at the house. He is so busy and spends most nights outside our house. The electric generator is running, but has a problem and is making a lot of noise. Azzam goes out to check it and then he turns it off. He said that we need to call a technician to look at it in the afternoon. Life without the generator is unbearable. The electricity wasn't on all day yesterday except for a short period in the afternoon. The generator was on from three in the afternoon till one in the morning because Majed was studying late. Before we went to sleep we heard distant explosions that lasted for an hour or two; we didn't know the source of these explosions. Today we found out that there were military clashes in the Al Doura area in southern Baghdad. In the afternoon the technician came and fixed a small problem. "Alhamdu Li Lahh" (Arabic for Thank God). Life returned to the house, but the water was very cold. I had to wait for hours until it was warm enough for me to wash my hair. I was wondering how people who don't own a generator take baths.

At night the darkness is frightening. We no longer go out to restaurants or visit friends or relatives in the evening. Even the phone lines haven't been repaired in the areas where they were bombed by the American army. As a result, there are no visits, no phone calls, and no strolls around Baghdad. Then again, what would I see? I would get sad and depressed. I would see a city run down by war. In every street you can see the remnants of a bombing or fire. Who did this? The foreigners or the locals? The American military is everywhere. The soldiers wander around the street with machine guns pointed at our faces. They ride the streets with their tanks when they need to. All the streets are cracked as a result. I see a different Baghdad, a Baghdad I didn't know before; a humiliated and occupied Baghdad. The same goes for the people. And then there are the checkpoints, slow traffic, lights flashed in our faces as if we were criminals. Sometimes an American soldier will ask us to get out of the car in the cold for inspection, then apologize politely and respectfully for disturbing us. I want to ask him, "What brought you to the end of the world, to Baghdad? Don't tell me you came here for our sake or to liberate us. Who will believe you? Do you believe it yourself?"

Everybody says we are not against the change; this is true, but we don't want it to happen like this. We hoped that change would come at the hands of Iraqis. It would have been more peaceful, beautiful, and joyful. But now everybody is against it. Who expects to wake up in the morning to see a foreign army, armed to their teeth filling our city? Had the change came from within, they would have found limitless support. We wouldn't have lost security and we wouldn't have witnessed the looting and executions. We would have seen an authority representing the people that is capable of restraining the masses. This authority wouldn't have allowed for revenge, laws would have been followed. The law is above everybody. It has been eight months since the fall of the regime and murders and executions are still occurring. Whoever has a list of names should hurry through it before a new government and constitution are formed. That is the reality today. We won't forget the opposition parties that were abroad and now are getting revenge at the symbols that bothered them in the past. Anyway, I think that the war crime trials that will be held later will find that all the accused have already been executed. This is the new justice in Iraq; our new freedom. Welcome!

Faiza Al-Araji

I spent last night in my family's house. Everyone looked very moody and grumpy. Khaled was having problems with university girls, Majed was studying for his religion examination, mom was typing more and more diaries on her PC, and my father was reading.

The explosions happened at midnight, and no one had enough energy even to wonder what was happening, but the breaking news at Al-Jazeera TV said American fighters were bombing AdDora, where one of my uncles lives. My father decided to call them and see what happened, but they were sleeping. My cousin said, "They are using cluster bombs, and we can hear the sound of a 57 (an Iraqi anti-aircraft gun) shooting back, but everyone here is sleeping."

There was street fighting today in Ad Dora, too. Naseem—the guy working in the internet café—was telling me about the Fedayeen attacking American troops. "There were dozens of them." I was surprised to discover some sites posting pictures and speeches about the resistance!

Raed Jarrar

My family is one of the very few, perhaps the only, family in Baghdad that is equipped with mobile phones. There was a special network established for NGOs (non-governmental organizations), and I was working with an NGO that my brother and father had established; as a result, we got phones to communicate with each other. The only problem is there is not enough electricity in Baghdad to charge your phone.

Khalid Jarrar

THURSDAY, DECEMBER 25, 2003

There are some positive aspects to this war. Most houses now have satellite dishes installed that receive transmissions from all over the world. Baghdad is full of Internet cafés and mobile phone dealerships, and we now find brand new cars of all models roaming the streets of the city. There are also many foreigners here now and their presence, whether as part of NGOs or foreign media and press, has broken the barriers we had with the outside world; we have found a common language for dialogue after I had thought such a language was impossible to find! I have discovered that there are many ordinary people among them and others that are intellectuals. When the American forces first entered into Baghdad they were kinder and cooperative with us, but now because of the security situation they have become more hostile, which has made people resentful of their presence, particularly after many Iraqis were accidentally shot dead by Americans because a soldier panicked! And of course who will bring that soldier to justice? These kinds of accidents brew a sense of resentment towards the Americans.

At night we hear explosions that go on for hours and nobody knows what's going on. We also hear helicopters flying around and the sound of tanks rumbling by breaking the quiet of the night and shaking the houses like miniature earthquakes. People are struggling to find food. Petrol, oil, and gasoline are scarce and very expensive, while during the long years of sanctions they were dirt-cheap. The mood of the people is not specifically due to these things but is an indication of the state of a nation that has been thrown into chaos and turmoil. And the future is unknown. The people who live here have tired of wars, sanctions, politics and political parties, and they wonder who will guarantee that the new faces are more sincere than those that have passed? The common language on the street is not one of forgiveness and national dialogue; rather, it is a language of vengeance and settling of old vendettas precisely like what the Ba'athists did to the Communists when they came into power. People here need a long time to learn to respect other peoples' opinions without resorting to violence or vengeance. This is a learning process and will be a result of a decision issued by one party or another.

Faiza Al-Araji

I have nothing personal against the soldiers here or against American civilians in the U.S. I have no doubt that most them really wanted to help and to do something good for this country and for the Iraqi people. But what I want to say is that some people with suits and large desks in the White House and other places are *not* that nice and sincere.

Let's say that Russia occupied your country (which just happens to be a really rich country with oil and other resources) and destroyed the country, killing civilians. Used cluster bombs and chemical weapons (for those of who don't believe the Americans have used chemical weapons, believe it or not, I have pictures of the dead bodies). Destroyed houses. Looted the whole governmental system, including the ministries, the police stations, fire departments, and airports. And afterward, they start a new newspaper, TV, and radio station, and begin telling you how happy you should be and how grateful you must be to them for liberating you. And later on, they put the pictures of your country's president (it doesn't matter whether you hate him or not) on TV with people checking his teeth. Now, take a moment, close your eyes, and look out the window. Now imagine that everything you see is destroyed. Every place you love is either bombed or looted. Everyone you love is probably dead or injured. Add to that very cold weather, no electricity, no gasoline. Now open your eyes and tell me: Does it really matter if the soldiers or their families are kind people?

Khalid Jarrar

FRIDAY, DECEMBER 26, 2003

I visited the neighbors today. The lady told me she wants to leave and sell the house. All her children live abroad and life here is difficult with no sign of improvement in the near future. She is right. I wish I could think like her, then all my problems would be over. But I am too attached to this land. Despite all the trouble and disaster, I love my country and would accept no substitute.

We have an apartment in Amman and right before the war broke out my husband suggested that the kids and I stay there until the war ends. We were on vacation at the time and I rejected the idea completely. The thought of the war taking place while I was away from Iraq drove me crazy and I hurriedly returned to Baghdad. It is a matter of principle! Many people ridiculed my decision; even my sisters called me a hopeless romantic, but I stuck to my decision and have no regrets. I told them I had not been there with them during any of the previous wars and I felt guilty for that. I also had a hunch that this would be Iraq's final war, and I had to share the experience of war first hand with my family, neighbors, and friends; therefore, I decided to remain in Baghdad and not to leave whatever the circumstances. Besides, what is there to live for if you all die and I am still alive? What would I do?

Those who experience the war have higher spirits than those living abroad listening to the news while worrying sick over friends and family. I have experienced that feeling before during the Iraq-Kuwait war while I was living in Amman. I cried daily worrying about my family and loved ones in Iraq. Being there with everyone during wartime is a mercy; consoling each other, laughing at the status quo, and hoping to live to tell the stories.

The early days of the war were easy on the people. The main targets were presidential and the army. Then the airborne attacks bombed targets in residential areas and this is when disaster struck. Days and nights became frightfully scary, and fear prevented us from going to sleep. The first night I took some valium and slept like the dead, but with time the valium stopped being effective and the intensity of the raids did not subside. The whole house would shake and the windows would break and we'd have to board them up. We'd wake up in the morning with headaches from pain and worry. Many families left their houses for areas far from Baghdad, but they were also haunted with the fear that their houses would be burgled or destroyed by the strikes. That was until the day the U.S. forces entered Baghdad airport; that day was a living hell for most residents of the capital, and we all left our houses to stay with relatives living far from the airport area.

I still think and wonder what Saddam was betting on when he sacrificed us into that hell! Only God knows how we survived those days, hearing news of raids on locations where military leaders 'supposedly' were, where innocent civilians were killed instead, which is precisely what happened during the strike at the Al-Sa'a restaurant in Al Mansour at around three in the afternoon when the street was packed with people walking about thinking they'd be safe during daytime hours. The buildings shook from the intensity of the attack; windows broke and houses were demolished on the families trapped inside. Those were dark days and we don't know who takes responsibility for them. Both sides lay blame on each other, and no one pays the price but us. We still do. And I cannot stand like an idiot and forget all we saw and idiotically applaud the occupying army.

Faiza Al-Araji

SUNDAY, DECEMBER 28, 2003

It is eight o'clock in the morning; outside it is raining and we have heavy fog. Yesterday I got several e-mails. I appreciate all of them regardless of whether they are encouraging or critical. I wish to thank everybody who wrote about their concern for us; it helps us get through the pain when we know that there are people around the world who care about us. The world has become a small village and a common dialogue is possible as long as we don't think in a selfish way. Thank you all.

I think of all the looting and crime that didn't exist before the war, at least not to the extent it does now. I think that the American army has unintentionally introduced these new concepts to us. The American army broke open the doors to the presidential palaces and invited everybody to come in and take a look inside. I know many poor and needy families but they didn't do such a thing, because they found it to be a shameful act that they would regret for many years to come. I know other families that were not poor and were not oppressed by Saddam; on the contrary, they were benefiting from the Saddam regime. These people couldn't wait to start looting and they were happy about it.

There is an Arabic proverb that says, "People follow the religion of their kings." The leader led by example. When the regime fell, the American army became the leader and the example. They allowed these idiots to loot and the army didn't realize that things would get out of hand very quickly. When they were finished looting state property, these people started to loot their fellow citizens.

Now with the shortage of gasoline, the American forces are distributing leaflets asking people to buy gas from the gas stations only and not from the black market. There are very strict penalties for people who don't comply, yet nobody is paying attention to these leaflets and people continue to buy gas on the black market. Do you know why? Because when you come in on the first day and you allow people to steal and loot, it becomes difficult for people to listen to you when you take on the role of the party that is dispensing advice.

Had an Iraqi party removed the regime, none of this would have happened, because they would have preserved everything. Not because they loved Saddam, but because they would have realized that these treasures belong to their country and they must look after them. They would have realized that all state property must be kept and can't be squandered away like it was. They would have urged the people to stand united and act in a reasonable way in such a strenuous situation, because unless we stand together and act rational we won't be able to get through this crisis.

Of course, there is another party that encouraged these foolish acts: the opposition parties that came from abroad riding on American tanks into our city. I also accuse our Kurdish brothers from the north, the area named Kurdistan. Kurdistan is now full of these stolen state cars. Some cars were stolen form storage places, and others by force from their owners. Some car owners were killed in the process. These cars are now being sold at auction. Maybe the owner's soul is hovering over its car. I wonder why people commit such evil acts. Why don't they say, "I can secure my daily bread and other necessities without spilling somebody's blood." The Kurdish people in the north are crying and complaining that they have been oppressed and killed by Saddam, so why do they allow the same thing to happen? If I criticize my enemy for being unjust and committing foolish acts, and if I act like them when I am in their place, how am I any better?

Another issue is the killing of previous Ba'athists without any due process and no questions asked. More that half of Iraqis were members of the Ba'ath party. How many Ba'athi will get his day? How many have their names of the list? How many Ba'athi were killed in front of their wives and children? When is this inhumanity going to end? The fools are fighting one another; in the end we all lose.

Faiza Al-Araji

MONDAY, DECEMBER 29, 2003

It is now five in the evening. I just finished doing the laundry since we have electricity. The electricity situation has improved in that last two days. We get electricity for three hours and then it goes off for several hours. In the days before the war I used to dry in the laundry in the drier. Now the drier is broken and it takes several days for the clothes to dry. The gasoline crisis is starting to get better. The rations are increasing for the gas stations and they are staying open for longer hours. Although the rations are set, the gas station attendant will fill your gas tank full and take something for his pocket. Who worries about principles these days except the fools? This is the state of the world. Now we wait at the gas station for only three hours instead of the whole day.

Yesterday I filled half the gas tank (100 liters) for 38,000 dinars. Last year I used to fill the whole tank (200 liters) for 5,000 dinars. I can afford it; but for others who don't have a good source of income or set salary, what do they do?

In the morning I went to pay the store's rent for the whole year of 2004. That is what the store owner requested. He asked for a 20% increase in rent from all the renters in all his buildings all over Iraq. I discovered that the owners are brothers from a wealthy family. Most of them own business buildings or are merchants.

The office was full of renters and all of them were complaining that they don't get much business and are not earning that much money. The employee of the owner was apologizing and telling everybody that it is not his fault, he is simply following the instruction of his bosses. He said he tried to pressure the owners to help the people but the owners refused because they are investors and their investments must grow. The war? They say it doesn't concern them! Whom does it concern then? This oppression has become fashionable. What is happening to the world?

Faiza Al-Araji

TUESDAY, DECEMBER 30, 2003

In the morning Raed traveled with Salam Pax to Amman Jordan to spend the New Year. I don't blame them, things here are boring; bombings, road blocks, electricity blackouts, long lines at the gas stations. Some good news though. It is the end of 2003. the year of the war, destruction and ruin, and the year of the end of the Saddam regime after 35 years. Who would have believed that? It is a miserable end to him and a miserable end to us. We are still living in an environment of war and its results. Another close bombing has just shaken the windows. We no longer ask each other, "What happened?" We just ask, "did you hear the explosion?"

The electricity was on for two hours then it went off for four; I consider this to be a good thing, as it is better than no electricity at all. Today something great happened that made me happy: the phone lines started working again! We are going back to square one, back to pre-war conditions. The phone switch at Al Ma'amoon was bombed at the beginning of the war and now a new building was set to house the phone switch in a nearby area. We can call people on the same phone switch. Later on when they connect with other phone switches we will be able to call other areas.

Faiza Al-Araji

WEDNESDAY, DECEMBER 31, 2003

It's the last day of 2003; it was hell of a year. I had to cancel my after-school lectures for today; students were either afraid of leaving their homes, or were warned by their parents of going out. Many rumors say that today some suicide bombers are going to *celebrate* the New Year.

From the very first moment I woke up at 7:00, I heard nonstop bombing and machine guns. I felt that this was just another day of the war. I went to school and found the school almost empty.

I had this important meeting with the managing board of the *Al-Muajaha* paper. Wassif's, the Editor-in-chief of the paper was shot in his leg a week ago during a pro-Saddam demonstration. We drew up some important new outlines about *Al-Muajaha* and its policy, and we decided to start printing issues and doing reports again after a four-month long break due to a lack of funds. Finally, we got some funding from "un Ponte per" (an Italian NGO; the initials stand for "A Bridge to" in English). So starting in February, *Al-Muajaha* will hopefully be back on track.

I finished the meeting with the other folks at about 4:00 and I headed home. I should have been home before 4:30, but the roads were all blocked because of several large explosions (one was nearby the newspaper offices and I saw a burned U.S. Humvee), so I didn't get home until 5:45.

I was invited to a small party at my aunt's, but I could not make it because of the roadblocks. Moreover, we could not even go out to have dinner for the same reason. Anyhow, it is two hours before the New Year now, and instead of chilling out and dancing with my girlfriend at a New Year's Party, I am instead writing this blog, feeling this hatred burning inside me.

It has been nine months since the terror broke out and things are still getting worse. The majority of Iraqis still thinks that Saddam was better than the U.S. authorities here. Promises were made, speeches were made, money was spent, and contracts were signed. But, I'm still living in a country where looters and killers have more freedom that I do; where the very simple basics in life are not available; where civilians get killed because soldiers are not careful handling their weapons; where people are not allowed to voice their opinions in the public media for fear that they may "inflame the passions against the coalition forces." I am not living in the same country I used to live in a year ago. I am not living in the country I hoped it would be. I am not living in the country that I was promised I would live in, but nonetheless, thank God, I *am* still living. That is reason enough to be liberated, isn't it?

In the morning the streets were jammed and we were hardly able to get to the store; even the side roads were very busy as well. Police, roadblocks, news about bombs planted in the streets, this is how the last day in Baghdad was spent. I imagine the other capitals around the world. I imagine people shopping in stores and celebrating in their homes, and here we are sneaking into our homes to hide.

When I passed through Baghdad's streets, I wondered to myself, why are the houses, hospitals, schools, and even the state buildings so old and run down? Supposedly, we a rich country. Where did the money go? We are an oil-rich country, right?

Look at our neighboring Persian Gulf states, look how their people live. They live very comfortably. The latest technologies have reached them and they don't worry about war or sanctions. Why are we buried in this backwardness and oppression? Why are we so distant from the rest of the world? People here always say that America brought Saddam Hussein into power so that he would destroy us. America supported him. All Iraqi attempts to get rid of him had failed. Then when America wanted to get rid of him, they came here to occupy Iraq. This had been their goal for decades. Whoever sees the army and tanks filling Iraq's cities would say, "Who is going to make them leave?" You can't believe that they will leave in a year or two; they will probably say they are staying here forever.

Saddam plundered the state's wealth from oil exports in order to wage wars for delusional reasons. The results of these wars has been nothing but destruction and ruin. Then came his war against Kuwait, who were our friends and neighbors. He found ridiculous reasons again to wage a war and who was going to stand up to him? We found out later what happened to people that stood up to him. He surrounded himself with a chorus of hypocrites that applaud anything he says and have no problem abusing poor helpless people.

The rest of the world kept distancing itself from us more and more, especially after the catastrophe of the sanctions. After the wars and the beginning of the sanctions, Saddam started putting his frustrations into wasting money on lavish palaces that he didn't live in, and in some cases, he never even visited. I used to see trucks in the evening full of young men wearing wretched clothing. These young men would sit there in the trucks. I would ask, "Who are these young men?" They were construction workers, working on the palace of the president. I would remember his famous expression, "O great nation of Iraq." I would say, "So these are the sons of the great nation of Iraq, building a palace for the great president." Really, I wonder who brought him to destroy us and wipe dignity from our lives. Could he have done this on his own? Or were there external powers that aided him and pressured him toward all this foolishness?

We were living in Amman, Jordan when Saddam attacked Kuwait. I said he is leading us to another hell after the end of the war with Iran. My coworker said, "Why are you upset? He is not doing anything to benefit himself, this will all benefit the people." I was very surprised by what he said. What benefit could come from oppressing other people and killing them? I didn't argue with him. I thought maybe I was stupid and I didn't have the same long-term vision. After the war on Kuwait and the sanctions, many Iraqis went abroad because they lost hope that things would get better. The countries of the world got our intellectuals, authors, artists, poets, doctors, and engineers; only very few stayed behind. So much so, that the Iraqi university had a shortage of teaching staff. Good thing new graduates were able to fill the empty positions. It felt as if the state was saying to the people, "Good bye and don't come back," unless you are willing to join those who support Saddam."

During this time I returned to Iraq. My family disagreed with my move and they asked, "What brought you here, you crazy woman?" I laughed and said, "God wanted me to come and he arranged the right circumstances in order for me to come, so don't try to persuade me otherwise." I came back to a destroyed country. All our values have eroded and all the people that were symbols of nationalism have died. The education system was corrupted, full of bribes. The health sector was ignored. The poor died due to a shortage of medicine and nobody cared about it. The rich were getting richer and the poor were getting poorer. The people started to sell their furniture and then gradually began selling their necessities. They even sold their fans and air conditioners during the summer just so that they could live. What kind of life is this? Retired government employees, army soldiers, and school teachers became an underclass. A new class emerged that had money, ran businesses, and owned the rights to import and export goods. This class of people was controlling the lives of everybody else. You would look at them and ask what qualifications do these people have, what degrees or skills? And the answer would be nothing. He is a friend of Mr. Uday or a relative of Mr. President.

Faiza Al-Araji

THURSDAY, JANUARY 8, 2004

I have had a headache since yesterday. Maybe it is because the electric generator has been broken in the store since Saturday. We tried to fix it but couldn't, so we sent it to a specialized center for repair. Maybe I will get it back on Saturday. I haven't surfed the Internet these past days. I just run to the nearest Internet café to read my e-mail and answer them. My e-mails are full of mistakes and spelling errors, but I don't worry about it. I hope that people reading my e-mails can do the corrections while they read. The electricity goes down and I lose all my writing; I get so depressed when that happens. So I rush to write again and send e-mails. I reread my e-mails and laugh at my own stupidity but it is too late, the e-mail has been sent.

Today I will talk again about our happy life after the liberation of Iraq. As soon as we become excited about the availability of electricity it gets worse again. We ask what happened. We get no response, of course. We are fed up with the explanations and excuses.

The same with the gas stations. The lines get better for a day or two but then they get worse again. The American army and their helicopters never stop with their escapades, day and night. The news is not good, except what the newspapers print about the optimistic expectations.

This morning I was driving my car around the airport area on my way to work. I was elated because my car had been in the garage for six months. As usual there was a group of American trucks driving along the way. Without meaning to, I ended up driving in the middle lane between them. The left lane was empty. I was afraid to pass the American trucks because they usually get annoyed and start shooting at you. I didn't want to put myself at risk, so I stayed in the middle lane. Then, I noticed that the soldier driving in the truck in front of me was nervously gesturing to me with his hand to get into the left lane. Then I noticed in my rear view mirror that other American army trucks were changing lanes and were now behind me. I guess I got the soldier upset and that is why he gestured to me like that. I got nervous so I changed lanes quickly to pass them. I felt that this soldier was rude and disrespectful. I am the daughter of this city, this land is where I live; this is the land of my forefathers, and then this stranger comes here and he becomes the master. He owns the street and I have to drive according to his instructions. Otherwise, he will very easily shoot me. He would find a thousand excuses for his actions. If my family filed a complaint against him, it would turn out that it was me who was at fault. They will say that I died as a result of my foolishness and bad judgment. But he, on the other hand was on a great mission to liberate Iraq. Therefore any Iraqi that is an annoyance to an American soldier is an obstacle to the accomplishment of the desired mission.

Yesterday I was listening to the news on one of the satellite stations. I heard about the dismissal of some American soldiers because they had beaten up Iraqi prisoners; they hit them on their head and genitals. I was shocked. They said that a sergeant confessed that she kicked the prisoner in his head and stomach with her military boots. I don't know what is more shocking, the fact that this

American woman hit the prisoner or that she is capable of such inhumanity and cruelty. Didn't the people that sent her here give her a brief lesson on the treatment of prisoners of war, or did they tell her, you are the master there, the decision maker, these people are worthless so do as you like sweetie. And then I wondered who reported this incident. Was it the poor prisoner? Or one of the sergeant's friends who still had some humanity and compassion left in him? The former is unlikely because who would listen to a despised prisoner; maybe he was a Ba'athist insect, so let him go to hell.

I immediately remembered a documentary that aired on one of the satellite stations that showed an Iraqi security officer kicking an arrested Iraqi. So what changed? Only that the shoe doing the kicking went from a locally made one to an American made one. I don't want to be a pessimist, but I have to admit that it is a big achievement; the improvement in the quality of the kicking shoe, I mean.

Today Mr. Bremer said in a news release that they will release some Iraqi prisoners today, others in batches later. He had one of the members of the Governing Council with him. This GC is a point of lots of debate; some accuse them of conspiring with the foreigners and others applaud in encouragement. In reality, I haven't seen any of the supporters yet; I only read about them in the opposition party newspapers. These newspapers, along with the American press, give the impression that everything is going just fine. There is only a small group of troublemakers that are causing problems. We need to get rid of them and then we can proceed with the reconstruction. I am afraid that in reality they want to clear the Iraqi streets of every critical mind and opposing spirit, including mine.

As for the members of the GC, I am not going to say that they are traitors and agents of a foreign power; I want to be reasonable and discuss their position objectively. They are a group of wealthy intellectuals and children from well-known families. They disappeared from the previous regime for whatever reason and went abroad to look for support. Under the banner that, "The enemy of my enemy is my friend," their interests happened to agree with the interests of the American government to change the regime. These people will get priority when important positions in the new government are doled out in return for acceptance of the American plans. All matters will be decided that way starting with the constitution, the army, the economy, and everything else. So the matter is clear, the GC is nothing but a symbolic presence with a limited function. In other words, the GC wouldn't be able to object because they will appear unappreciative of the favor. That is the point of obligation that can't be infringed upon. Because they believe that they were the prosecuted opposition in the past, they have the right to be in the front leading us now. A dream come true, the good positions and the fat business deals, for them, their family, and their friends.

Mr. Bremer says that the coalition forces will not release those who participated in committing crimes against the Iraqi people. This foolish lady that lives inside me asked, "What about all the Iraqi civilians that were killed by the coalition forces during the air strikes or after the fall of the regime?" The instructions were to shoot any moving target when they entered Baghdad and other cities. The result? Hundreds of civilians murdered in their cars because they were moving targets. In came the American NGOs to tally up the dead and injured and they promised the bereaved families compensation from the American government, then the NGOs left and didn't come back. Then came the press and TV stations from America and Europe and they wrote about cluster bombs and their effect on people and children, especially the children. They left and didn't come back. They didn't do a thing for the families of the victims. Were they serious or just having fun in order to fill their papers with stories? Who takes responsibility for the spilled blood? Or is this blood worthless because it is not American? It doesn't deserve the trouble to investigate.

The media is a weapon more dangerous that firearms; they lie and cover up the truth. The people are ignorant of what is going on, busy with their daily lives. A small group of people control the whole world and does whatever suits them. They justify everything in the name of the people and the people don't necessarily know what is going on. It is all the same, here and there!

Faiza Al-Araji

TUESDAY, JANUARY 9, 2004

Haven't we passed the time of oppression with the fall of Saddam Hussein? We want to build our new democratic country, so why divide the house and the riches? Why isolate ourselves? Who loves Iraq? Who wants to see Iraq strong, united, and harmonious? Other people have other purposes. Only God knows the truth.

I am afraid that the occupation will create a reality on the ground that will be difficult to change later on. The occupation will leave behind a leadership that is favorable to it, that continues to implement its vision and purposes, even after the army has left. And then they will say, "Go ahead, have elections." Elections to decide what? If the essential matters have already been decided without involving the people, what is the point of having elections after the fact? Is this the democracy that we have been dreaming about for so long? Are we such an ignorant nation that we don't know what is in our best interest? Or is that the strangers can't stop meddling in our business and planning our future? What gave them the right to enter our house and make themselves masters of it?

And so the time passes. Some us are ignorant and support them; some of us are stupid and try to benefit from them; some of us are naïve and don't know what is going on; some of us are angered and throw bombs; and some like me are sad. A tear runs down my cheek, the sadness squeezes my heart. Why don't they leave us alone? Why can't we live in peace in a way that suits us?

Faiza Al-Araji

SATURDAY, JANUARY 10, 2004

Today I want to explore a new topic for discussion. As a result of many questions I got by e-mail, and in order to alleviate the boredom and depression, I decided to talk about something personal, about our daily life. All the schools are having mid-term exams. Usually these are tense times in our family. Each one of the kids is hiding in his room and you cannot expect any aid from them because they would just yell, "I have exams, leave me alone!" They stay up till late at night and wake up early to finish studying. I have to beg them to eat breakfast.

I stay worried all day long until they come back and then I feel relieved. And so we start again the next day, the thinking and worrying, what does tomorrow hold? When we are children we are just innocent and naive creatures. Then we learn and grow up. In our teens we become troublesome creatures for our families and ourselves. Then we grow up a bit and learn responsibility and we mature. We start to feel comfortable, we become confident and we gain inner peace. But our children stir this peace. So we start to worry about them and worry about their future. Now I remember my mom and dad; I feel all the pain that they lived through in order to raise us. All the troubles they had faced when they had limited income and many children. Azzam and I both work, so the income of the family is excellent, praise to God. We have worked very hard for what we have. The kids became involved with their studies; that is what made us decide to stay here. We are always trying to meet the demand of the home and the kids, and we are worried about the future. I think that people in the old days were more at ease and had more peace of mind. Life was calmer and safer. Life was less complex, people's dreams were simpler. We were eight kids, four girls and four boys. We studied and graduated from universities (Engineering, Medicine, Dentistry, and Pharmacy). It did not cost my family a thing because university was free. In the Eid Alsagheer (Muslim holiday) they would buy us new clothes, which we would put away to wear again in Eid Al Kabeer (another Muslim holiday), because their budget was too limited to purchase new clothing for both occasions.

My father used to own a bookstore In Baghdad's old market, in which he sold books and stationary. It was called Al Sarai market; it is still there till today. Our house was located near the market and so were the schools. Sometimes we would go to the store to help out. We would be shaking with fear when one of our teachers would walk into the store to buy pencils or notebooks from my dad, so we would hide under the table so the teacher wouldn't see us. We used to respect this greater-than-life figure called teacher, because that job was sacred. The teachers had lots of self-respect, they knew that their job held a big responsibility towards raising a generation and not just teaching kids to read and write.

Growing up, my dad kept his library in the basement. He had hundreds of books, stories and novels, historical and religious books, folkloric books and old songs. During the summer holiday we would go down into the library and sink into reading all these books. My poor mom would scream and yell because we wouldn't help her out with the housework. I always remember this when my kids give me a hard time now and I laugh. I tell myself, such is life. You torment your mother today and tomorrow your son will torment you. It is divine justice. My mom would spend the whole day doing the laundry, cooking, and cleaning the house. She had neither a servant to help her nor home appliances. She would wake up early in the morning to make us breakfast, then she would wake us up and help us get ready for school. Then she would go to the market to buy fruits, vegetables, and meat. That is what life was like in those days, and everybody found a way to live. I learned to be energetic from my mom, but I find myself to be spoiled compared to the women of the previous generation. They were deprived of education and work and had to dedicate themselves to housework. This has its own advantages and disadvantages. My mom would tell us you are better than me, because you went to school, you won't be prisoners of the authority of a husband and kids. They can become tyrants when they grow up. We didn't really understand what she meant, but then we grew up and witnessed the cruelty of the world. Life passes and everybody wants to fulfill his own ambitions without caring about others. We started to understand that it is beautiful to have our own dreams and ambitions. My generation is less likely to get depressed, because we don't feel like useless creatures that spend our time doing nothing. My mom and dad died many years ago, but I remember all the details of those days. I regret every advice they gave me that I didn't listen to. I regret each word I said to them in anger. I would argue with them with the enthusiasm and foolishness of my youth. Now I laugh at myself when my children become stubborn and argumentative. I tell them I used to be like you when I was your age. I, too, was stubborn and arrogant, I thought I was smarter than them all, just like you think now. How many things I thought were so beautiful that I exhausted myself in order to get them, only to discover that they are trivial illusions. How many years of your life will you spend running after a mirage until you grow up and stop this foolishness?

Now we live in a detached house with a big garden around it. The house has four bedrooms and sittings rooms, a dining room, a big kitchen, a storage room, and three bathrooms. There is a woman that usually comes in three times a week to help me clean the house. I need her help because time passes quickly and I don't have enough time to do everything. I go to work at the store before ten in the morning, and I get back home after two in the afternoon.

At the store we sell imported laboratory equipment used to test the quality of drinking water, which can also be used in factories or laboratories. We also sell water filters that can be used by individuals, organizations, governmental agencies, embassies, or hospitals. Many clients come to the store from all walks of life. I discuss the customer's needs when they come in. I help them choose a suitable piece of equipment. Sometimes I am busy writing acquisition requests or doing inventory management. When I am busy with other work I ask another engineer to deal with the customers and tell him that he can always come ask me questions if he has any problems.. I look after sales, inventory, and all the details of the daily business. We also have management staff and engineers working at the store. I like to think that we are like a family and not just coworkers at business. Because I am a woman, I like to be spoiled at work, which means I get the men to do things like taking care of the electric generator, the gas, the oil, pushing the heavy carts, paying bills, cleaning the pavement outside the store, and giving money to the beggars (there are so many). I gave instructions not to turn the beggars away. We have a set schedule for giving these people money, each group of beggars has a day of the week.

The neighbors always say that I am hiding. I always apologize because I am busy. When we do get together, they ask me to tell them the latest news, since they are locked up in the house. I tell them many different stories about what I have heard and seen in previous days. We laugh, drink tea, and eat pastry or cake. We discuss world affairs and politics. Sometimes we agree and sometimes we disagree. My neighbor to the left was a Ba'athist, as was her husband. They were very isolated; nobody liked them. Now they are even more isolated; we never see them. My neighbors to the right, most of their family was deported to Iran during the war with Iran. That was Saddam's great effort in solving problems. Also, their brother was executed. My neighbor to the right of her, her brother was executed by Saddam. The neighbor next to her, most of her brothers went abroad to escape Saddam because they were Communists. The people living behind us, their uncle was executed by Saddam, because he hosted a person belonging to the Al Da'awa party.

When work hours are over, I stop at many stores before I go home. I buy vegetables, fruits, cheeses, and breads. I take my clothes to be ironed and also buy things I need like shampoo or other cosmetics. Also I might need to repair a watch or exchange batteries, buy bedroom linens, towels, or other things that you only buy once in a while. I try to rush when I am shopping because I am usually hungry and lunch hour is near. After lunch I might go to sleep, read, or surf the Internet. In the evening, I either go visit one of the neighbors or I go with the driver to the market to go shopping for clothes and shoes. I might have to visit the doctor or get a haircut or visit one of my sisters. After eight in the evening we have dinner. We all gather together in front of the TV. The kids eat and laugh while watching TV. These are the happiest moment of my life. When the outside door is locked and the family gathers together, we are eating dinner and our number is complete. Nobody is outside and nobody is traveling somewhere. I think it must be the same for all the mothers of the world. That is why I hate wars; they rip families apart. I wish peace to the whole world and to all mothers. If it was up to women there would be no wars in the world because we love our husbands, sons, brothers, and fathers too much.

Faiza Al-Araji

Word of the day: *Privatizing.*

I remember myself giving a boring lecture about the socio-cultural changes in post-war Iraq, and since I'm such a bossy ego-centric freak, it didn't bother me much to see most of the poor sleepy Italian kids moaning and begging for a break.

I believe the war has two main goals: destroying the political regime and changing the economic system. Crushing the political structure is done and changing the economic one is still in process.

The first step in changing the socialist economical system was bombing some of the public/governmental-sector companies, and leaving the rest to be looted and burned in the weeks after. The second step of privatizing is happening at the time; it started some weeks ago. Small companies and parts of the public sector are being sold, some governmental companies belonging to the ministry of industry, some furnaces, some warehouses and stores, and some other small places that you can read advertisements about in our new daily newspapers.

Raed Jarrar

SUNDAY, JANUARY 11, 2004

Raed gave me an Arabic copy of the latest edition of *Newsweek*. There were many articles about the arrest of Saddam and the liberation of Iraq. One article in particular devastated me. Its title, "Sin in Iraq," mentioned the availability of houses of prostitution in the new Iraq. The article provides the exact locations and the prices. It talks about a new wave of liquor stores, drugs, and adult movie theaters. The article contained interviews with people who explained their happiness now because Saddam had forbidden such things.

In an interview with a policeman, the policeman said that there was nothing he could do to control the prostitutes because the occupation forces simply release them when they are arrested. Had this article been published in an anti-U.S. newspaper, I would have said that they were lying and making it all up. I have never seen or heard of something like this. Isn't it embarrassing that this magazine is published in the U.S. and read by the American public? Are they going to smile and laugh about this or are they going to feel embarrassment and say that they shouldn't be talking about this? They should say that they won't allow these transgressions to happen out of their respect for the Iraqi people and Islam; that is, if they came here as friends to help us, as they claim. If they came as enemies, this is exactly what they would do to expose their hypocrisy to the world.

The pictures with the article don't collaborate the claims made in the article. The people in the pictures are average citizens; one of them is holding a can of Pepsi, and another a bottle of Miranda (a soft drink). The dancing girls in the pictures work for a well-known national folk dance company.

The article states that Saddam used to forbid the sale of alcohol and would cut off the heads of prostitutes. I say this is a lie. Had he been straight and careful about religion and morals, God wouldn't have abandoned him. The Iraqi nation is waiting for an apology from the author of the article and the magazine itself. If they have respect for the journalism profession and their goals are noble, they should do just that. There are some that don't respect this profession and stains it with their inconsideration. Where was the senior editor when this article was published? How could he or she print such lies? I promise you, I won't be buying this magazine again, and I will tell every Iraqi to do the same.

Faiza Al-Araji

MONDAY, JANUARY 12, 2004

I get lots of e-mail. Most of the letters I get are nice, even when they come from Americans. Many of the people, both men and women, are sympathetic; they wish us well, and hope that we find a way to get through theses difficult days we are facing. The e-mails come from a wide range of ages, but most are from people in their forties. I also noticed that most of the e-mails that my children receive are hostile, especially when they come from kids their own age. They accuse my children of being Ba'athist or belonging to Hamas. To me this proves that these young inexperienced people are the victims of a dishonest western media, whereas the older and more mature people have the ability to decipher what they view in the media. I wish that mothers and fathers would direct their children toward a fairer way of thinking.

When Baghdad fell, many organizations started to operate inside Baghdad. Raed, Majed, and Khalid formed many friendships with foreigners. They would bring them home for lunch and dinner and we would sit together as if we were one family. The kids would treat them as their own siblings and Azzam and I would treat them as if they were our own children.

In every society there is a group of people that is closed off to the rest of the world and that is against exposure to other cultures. This is bad enough, but it gets worse when the media singles out a particular culture, like what is happening against Muslim countries. The media gives the impression that we are monsters that love explosives and terrorist organizations. Who will explain that we are not? Who will believe us?

Saddam tried hard to divide Iraqis and isolate one group from the other, Sunni and Shia, Kurdish and Arab. This is a hateful way to classify human beings who live in the same country and have common traditions and morals. So why do we forget all this and hold on to the one thing the divides us? Don't tell me that this holds a greater good. What good can come from divisiveness? Saddam failed to get the Iraqis to divide, but the danger now is greater. Chaos is the mistress of these times. Europe was able to unite after a history that has been stained with blood. The U.S. was united after the Civil War, and the tensions between whites and blacks. We on the other hand, are entering into this dark tunnel that others have left hundreds of years ago.

After I left work, I was buying fruits when I came across this poor lady. She used to work as a cleaner in a nearby building. I asked her about herself and about her children. She told me that she left work because of the safety situation; she is afraid to leave her home. She is waiting for the retirement pay from her late husband. I asked her when she was last paid, and she said that she got an installment before Eid Al Sagheir (Muslim holiday) that was during Ramadan (the holy month of fasting). Ramadan was two months ago! I inquired about the other installments? She said that she was told there is no money; perhaps in another month, maybe more. How does she live? She said she doesn't know. I can help this woman, but what about the hundreds and thousands of other families? Who will help them? I remembered a saying, "Like a poor camel that is eating dry prickly plants while carrying boxes of gold on his back." Isn't that the state of the Iraqi people that live atop an oil well, yet are hungry and unemployed? And you wonder why I have a headache?

Faiza Al-Araji

WEDNESDAY, JANUARY 14, 2004

I hesitated before publishing the post of January the 11th. To be honest, I wrote it when I was angry about what was going on. The media outlets are responsible somehow. People abroad don't know the truth about our daily lives. When I tried to publish it on the Web site I had some technical problems. I wavered and delayed publication till the next morning. I couldn't sleep that night. I was struck by a panic attack. I was afraid of the responses I would get. Are they going to be cruel? Each time I heard a helicopter passing by our house, I would imagine that they were there to drop a rocket on us. This is the house of those evil people that write the truth. Let's bomb them!

I prayed to God that if I was right, he would support me and help me out. I didn't mean to offend anybody, but I don't like to stay silent when I face an unfair situation. In the morning I was still worried but eventually found the courage to post it on the Web site. That evening I got 29 e-mails. One of them was ridiculing me but the rest were supportive, thanking me and apologetic about what we are going through. I spent most of the evening sending thank you e-mails. I am now more convinced that the world has become a small village and there is a common language for discussion among people of all nationalities. People from all around the world love peace and want safety for their children, family, and friends. Then there are these small wishes that we have. That we would dress well, eat well, and live life with dignity. We have hobbies and interests, we have friends that we love and we enjoy nature. We live in a peaceful way. We all agree on that. Then what is the point of war? What is the point of losing the people that we love? What do we benefit from ruining our lives and the lives of others?

Many of the people who sent me e-mails are mothers and fathers who want this war to end. They want their children to come home to them as soon as possible. I say we here, too, want this war to end and our sons and daughters to return to us. But the question is, who decides? Who is planning our future and your future? The people here and there want peace. But there are small groups here and there that have other interests. We, the majority, become the victims of the dreams of this minority. A minority that never gets enough deals, investments, and profits. Here and there, it is all the same. The people pay the price with their blood and their offspring's blood. The media is relentless in lying, justifying, and disfiguring reality. The young of age and experience are the victims of this; they become the fuel for these wars. It is easy to attract and deceive the young with slogans about country and distant dreams. It is easy to incite them against an enemy; convince them that life can't go on without eliminating this enemy. There will be no justice or truth on earth. There are always thousands of ears listening to such propaganda. Add some financial incentives and very quickly you are filling the graveyards of both countries with young people.

Is what Saddam did to us all that different than what other leaders do to their people? The same strategy, the same way of thinking. Who is paying attention? At what loss will these leaders stop committing this foolishness? Does it help to simply change the people at the top? Are there a limited number of men that are playing games with the destiny of nations around the world? Are these leaders just employees of these men?

Faiza Al-Araji

THURSDAY, JANUARY 15, 2004

I hate Saddam. He is a criminal. I didn't support him. I was against his government.

I am just trying to reduce the number of hate e-mails that I will get today; those who will start their message with, "You ungrateful Ba'athist."

So you cannot send me those e-mails today because I have already said that I hate Saddam.

Explosions are a part of our daily lives. It could be the only place in the world that people don't interrupt their conversations when something explodes nearby; it is something that we have learned to deal with.

Explosions are such horrible things. When you hear one, you realize that it means that someone lost a head, a leg, or a hand; someone lost his shop, his only way to support his family; someone lost his whole house. Boom! And just like that—a few seconds—changes the lives of those around forever.

Thanks to the liberation forces, we have had enough explosions to remember for the rest of our lives.

I said earlier that most of the e-mail I receive is from the States; nice people, mostly. I also receive nice mail from Canada, Australia, Brazil, Uruguay, the Far East, and the U.K. I am grateful that people from around the world share their opinions with me. I know that there is always something that we all can teach each other.

One of my e-mail friends from the states asked, "Should we, 'the Americans,' be concerned about what kind of rights the new government of Iraq will give to the minorities?" I was thinking, "Why the hell should we, 'as Iraqis,' care about the opinion of someone who lives 10,000 km away? About what kind of government we should have? Do the Americans think it's their right to make a government *here* that satisfies *their* standards? Why should they have a say in this?

Let me get this straight, they weren't happy about the government here, so they came *here* to change it and make a new one that *they* like? It's going to take years of watching *CNN* and *BBC* to understand that.

But here are the facts. It's been almost a year since the war began, and we still haven't seen any sign of the new promised land, the new Iraq. We still don't have half the life that we used to have. Will we ever have a government? We don't have electricity, we don't have security and we don't have gas. Our infrastructure has been destroyed, along with hundreds of buildings. This is the new Iraq!

Khalid Jarrar

FRIDAY, JANUARY 16, 2004

I remember the days before the war when people from the national-but-corrupted-and-arrogant-government were using the same smart propaganda to justify their loyalty to Saddam: "A civil war will start, no one can control this country, even if he isn't the best person in the world at least he is keeping the situation stable." The same excuse was given today, by Iraqis demonstrating at Basra.

Americans were supposed to hand over authority to the Iraqis next June, and discussions were about how and where and other details; this was announced after months of playing the (try and screw-up) game. The political hand-over was supposed to happen in the middle of this year, but the thing/government was not going to be elected, it was supposed to be (s-elected), preparing for the general elections in two years.

I have no doubts that Americans want to stay as long as they can in their current position, and I don't have any doubts "they" will try to use any excuse that can be found.

Tens of thousands of Iraqis demonstrated at Basra—the new Shia'a capital—today. But why? It was because of the new speech/fatwa of Ayat-Allah Sistani about the form of the next government.

Sistani is one of the key personalities in the "new" Iraq, (in fact he's one of the few leaders that used to live in Iraq before the war), he really controls millions of Shia'a in the south and they really believe in him. Americans treat him as a local god, giving him enormous self confidence and image.

Sistani refuses to accept the "elected government" phase; he wants to jump to the "general elections" stage without the intermediate one. Why? Because he doesn't feel safe! Because he believes Americans are giving him what he wants.

Sistani doesn't feel very safe having an ethnic-mixture-(American-free) government for the next two years (not very safe to go through all the discussions and crap of convincing dozens of representatives of different ethnic and religious groups that may dominate the political scene in the time that he can control everything by himself and have more respectful position during the presence of Americans or after the general elections will take place). But why would a person like him give Americans a fashionable excuse for staying for another two years?

Because they built up the scene this way: They gave him lots of attention and care, and then threatened to leave him. They knew he would then start begging for them to stay and this is how the Americans are justifying the reasons for their existence in Iraq.

People are repeating the same "we don't want a civil war" advertisement to justify Sistani's new position. But why? Does a person like him have an agreement with the Americans? I don't think so, it's more sophisticated than that. Are Americans happy because of his position? Yes, at least till now. Are Americans considering this as a favor? No, I doubt it. They don't have favors and permanent friends, they have permanent interests. Do Americans realize they are playing with fire? I don't think they do.

From a practical American point of view, Iraq is neither ready technically nor politically to start a general election. We are talking about a country that could not rebuild the services billing system until now.

Iraqis didn't pay a dinar for (the so-called) electricity, water, telecommunication stuff, and other public services for the last ten months, but not because Americans are trying to build a new communist era, it's because of the lack of capabilities of issuing bills!

We are speaking about basics here; small problems like traffic jams seem to be huge enough to be considered a challenge for the GC, so what do you expect to get when issues like general elections are discussed?

Otherwise, and from a political position, let's suppose this technical problem isn't that Americans will not give the situation a chance to get out of control and repeat the Algerian catastrophe, when the so-called (democratic general elections) will end up creating a new religious monster that might not be western-friendly.

The same way that I was sure that the Americans would not give Saddam Hussein a free passion-inflaming channel by starting a public trial, I can say that I'm positive Americans will not give Iraq neither as a Shia'a present to Iran nor a Sunni present to Saudi Arabia. General elections cannot even be discussed before Iraqis finish their cultural and political lessons. Teach them the neo-Islamic theory: Secular Islam(?).

Would it end up causing a mess? Would the impact cause extremely right winged groups? Would these "outsiders," who are putting more and more pressure to change the socio-cultural-religious common beliefs, be accepted?

I'm trying to be pragmatic and rational without forgetting the national context. I can understand that when Americans come to occupy a country, they will rebuild it in their way, but when issues like privatization, capitalism, federalism, open market policy, and an open telecommunication system come in one package, I don't see a point even in discussing their presence or not; it's stupid to feel surprised every time one of these topics pops up, but it's not stupid at all to discuss the methods and ways of reaching those main goals, sometimes methodologies are more harmful than the goals themselves.

Confusion is the keyword here.

I know the American army is not leaving Iraq for years, and I know American decision makers will not leave for decades.

Do you know that the American embassy in Baghdad will have more than 3000 "diplomats" working there? They are the next government, no doubt. Just announce it for God's sake; announce that and let's play a clean game.

Why must we go through this process of tearing up Iraq? Federalism, Shia'a, Sunnis, Turkmen, Kurds, Assyrians, picking a weak dependant governing council, with no roots, and threatening to leave after a year; of course they'll start whining and begging for the devil to stay.

Why didn't anyone ask us whether we wanted the war or not? Whether we felt comfortable with the GC or not? Why didn't anyone ask if the game of jumping from one plan to another with no vision is amusing or not? But everyone comes now and asks do you want "them" to leave or stay?

There is an Arabic proverb that says, "One hundred wise men are not enough to find the stone that the freak threw in the well."

You threw the stone, you find it.

Raed Jarrar

SUNDAY, JANUARY 18, 2004

Good morning. Then again, there have been explosions all morning, so what's good about it? These explosions are meaningless; they only result in loss of life. Who are the people who carry out these bombings, and who are the people who give the orders? I don't understand. Maybe there's another language in the world with a vocabulary that includes killing and blood and innocent victims.

I get amazing e-mails from people all around the word: India, Italy, France, Holland, Norway, and different states in the U.S., like New York, Massachusetts, California, and Michigan. All the e-mails I get are full of warmth and understanding for our situation. They even say the blog about our everyday lives is similar to their own family life, and their memories are like my own! These letters make me so happy! I always thought it would take hundreds of years for us to meet and understand each other but I'm finding that we are all simple humans who have more in common than we have differences, despite the distance between us, our cultures, and our religions. It makes me wonder why our governments aren't more like us. I'll never know the answer.

Let's get back to Baghdad. The electricity is better, but it might be worse again when I blog tomorrow or the day after; nobody knows.

91

The lines in front of the gas stations are shorter, for now. The dollar is improving, especially after the scandal of the airplane loaded with 20 billion new Iraqi dinars in Beirut Airport.

By the way, who is going to investigate this scandal and punish the bad guys? In the past, during Saddam's days, the Western media specialized in publicizing Saddam's scandals. Well, today, who is going to care about us? And who do we complain to? Only God. The retirement wages have been postponed, as have the wages of the former army. There are no employment opportunities in the country, just explosions and raids upon homes for fear that someone is hiding weapons. These raids usually occur at night, and are often the result of an Iraqi's tip-off to American forces about his neighbor or relative or someone who means nothing to him. They pay the informer money (a reward for his good work). A couple of days ago, I heard a story about one of these raids. The wife said they blew up the main wooden door with a small bomb in the middle of the night. The woman and her son ran to hide under the staircase in terror. The troops went to the kitchen where the woman's husband was located, tied him up, put a bag over his head and took him away. After five days, they dropped him off in the dead of night on a street near his house. He eagerly returned to his family, and told them that after they removed the bag from his head, they interrogated him, asking for his name, his job and other things, and then they let him go.

His wife was crying and saying, "We're leaving. I won't stay here anymore!" And I'm wondering who will defend us when we complain? Who will believe us? Who will uphold our rights and our dignity while we are under the occupation of a country that boasts it is a country of freedom? Can't a door be knocked on during the day and questions asked with a little less hostility? Without breaking down doors and putting bags over heads, which the victims keep to prove to themselves and to us that it wasn't just a nightmare, but a reality.

Faiza Al-Araji

Did you see the explosion of the day? God damn it! Today, the number of American soldiers killed in Iraq reached 500.

But no one even mentioned that; it was the "Bremer Dinar" scandals day. The Iraqi Dinar lost 50% of its value overnight, after discovering that our CG is selling billions of dinars to the world under the brand new operation called "screw up yourself, your neighbors, and your national currency." I would like to take this chance to thank our great GC for their great policies in giving more trust in the Iraqi Dinar and the Iraqi economy.

Secular Muslim is my favorite way in describing me. When I discuss the issues of religion and culture with myself, we never fight.

Islam is that huge heritage of architecture (my grandfather's courtyard house), music (um kalthum and fayrooz), food (doolma and yabsah), colors (green palm trees and brown bricks), language (my love letters and quraan), poems (Sayyab and Motanabbi), books (Jaaberi and Kanafani), smell and taste (bakhoor and hareesa), chai (abo el heel and noomi al basra), quraan (mosques and harmony), and me.

Maybe that's why we can't drop that heritage or hand it over easily to other people with long beards just because they are religious and me and I am anti-religious. I mean, what would be the point? I don't believe in the Islamic religion, but I am a part of the Islamic culture and society. My ex-girlfriend told me once, "Raed, you try to treat me in a modern way, but from deep inside I can feel the Islamic system in you."

I belong to the big secular family, and all this crap about religion doesn't move a hair on my body (it's an Arabic expression).

But unexpectedly, the thing that made most of the hair on my head stand was when I heard the news about France and Belgium taking these ultra-stupid-shallow-decisions of veil/hijab.

I find myself forced to criticize my secular tribe! What the hell are you doing there? This is not supposed to be *our* part of the game.

I lived in Saudi Arabia for four years, in a small city in the south called Abha. And there the medieval, shallow, corrupted government used to send religious men called "mtawwe" to insure that all women cover their bodies and look like black tents. I remember my mother—the sophisticated feminist engineer—putting that black thing on her, covering her head and face, to the point that no one can tell in which direction she was facing. These are the people whom *we* (me and my secular cousins) must teach how to live and understand life.

Did French people decide to hate freedom after McDonald's changed the name of French fries to freedom fries? Is it envy then?

I mean how did you decide to go and run after women to take off the stupid piece of cloth on their heads? What is the point?

Isn't a punk allowed to come to school with his or her hair dyed red? Isn't a Goth allowed to come with his black eyes? Why do you start another battle between cultures out of nothing?

Doesn't the UN crap speak about freedom of beliefs? Isn't that what *we* are trying to convince the rest of the world?

Don't words like discrimination pull any triggers here?

Shame on you!

Raed Jarrar

MONDAY, JANUARY 19, 2004

The explosion in front of the Presidential palace two days ago happened on the 13th anniversary of the 1991 war, the war that destroyed everything, but left the rest of Iraq and her neighbors to be milked slowly.

Today's demonstrations in Baghdad were a bit huge, and people were shouting "Yes for elections, Yes for democracy," "No for those who came from outside to rule us."

When the situation was building up slowly in the south, no one even noticed them. All the focus was on attacks happening in the middle region of Iraq.

Who's the most irresponsible of them all? Will the Americans give Shia'a their democratic elections in the south? Of course not.

Raed Jarrar

THURSDAY, JANUARY 22, 2004

Today was a special day.

Here I am in my family's house, drinking vodka alone at three in the morning. One year ago I was staying in Amman, waiting for my visa to go to Saudi Arabia to marry my first love and ex-fiancé. I was finishing my studies for my Masters Degree, and I was working as an architect in a small engineering office.

I will not exaggerate and pretend this is my first jump between my parallel universes, because I had previous heroic hyper-jumps in the past.

But this year witnessed two jumps.

Jump, Raed. Jump. Jump. Jump.

The first was on the 19th of February of last year, when I decided to leave my work, my house, and to leave Heba and come to Iraq.

This is when everyone starts to wonder, "Where is Raed?"

I came to Baghdad; I was completely destroyed; I had no energy. I slept all day and night waiting for the war to start, to use as the "reason" for my miserable life. The war started and the explosions helped me to forget the rest of my feelings toward Heba. The war stopped, and statues were pulled down in a dramatic way.

My patriotic feelings pushed me to start something that can make the world see how bad this war is, so I started working on a massive scale survey on war casualties, for months, going on trips to the nine cites of the south weekly, and establishing a huge network of volunteers, monitoring them, designing the survey forms, and administering the data input procedure.

More than 4,000 injured, more than 2,000 killed, and that's just civilians, all with full documentation and details about the time and place of incidents and their addresses.

After we finished the survey, I started establishing another network of volunteers—Emaar—in the nine cities of the south and Baghdad. One hundred volunteers were the result of a one month selection period in which I met around 1500 persons, around 30 of the 100 were girls, working all together in teams to identify small problems in the neighborhoods and implementing small projects depending on the local people's contribution, to give them more trust in themselves and to market the political idea of giving Iraqis the chance to rebuild their countries by themselves.

Meanwhile I had a romantic story that was getting more serious day by day, and making me a worse person day by day, too.

After the UN explosion, fund raising started being impossible, and our only agency stopped funding us for political reasons. My private life was falling apart in parallel to Emaar, slowly and painfully. Even working with Salam, for the *BBC*, and writing stuff on this blog wasn't making me comfortable. For many reasons.

Today was a special day. I stood in front of everyone in the NGOs meeting, and told them, "I'm sorry to announce the death of Emaar in 9 of the 10 governorates that we used to work in." We still have work in the marshes of Nasiriya.

I'm tired, and I cant knock on any more doors. The teams in Nasiriya are arranging themselves without my help. Good for them.

I e-mailed the Jordanian University to tell them I'm not going to resume my Masters Degree studies. It's way too complicated for me now. I'll take my diploma certificate and stop.

And I e-mailed a friend in London telling her about my great achievements today. I burned myself out.

Today was a special day, but this Russian vodka made it better.

Jump, jump, jump.

Raed Jarrar

MONDAY, JANUARY 26, 2004

This morning, before I went to work, I checked my e-mails and found seven letters all asking about Raed: Was he ok? I didn't understand. What was happening?

I went back and checked his page on the internet and found he had written about some very depressing thoughts he was having. I understood now why those people had sent those concerned letters.

Of course by "jump, jump," he meant he wasn't settled; jumping from one job to another and from one set of circumstances to another. Apparently, some people thought he might actually "jump" from the roof of a building!

I said, "Oh God, not again!" Ever since he graduated from college, he goes through this phase almost every six months. Of course, I live it with difficulty and pain because he won't let anyone get involved. He wants to weather his experiences alone and I'm afraid he'll do something extreme. Like commit suicide or take drugs. By the time the emotional trauma is over, I've usually spent all of my energy coping and being patient and I can feel the beginnings of an emotional breakdown. I hide in the house and don't want to see anyone and don't want anyone to see me.

So Raed's depression becomes my depression, and the question poses itself: What is the meaning of my insignificant life? I think we're all prone to that, even when we stay strong for other people and hide our weaknesses. Sometimes while laughing and saying something like, "When I'm depressed...," people will interrupt me and say, "You? Depressed? That's impossible!" So I wonder, why? They tell me I'm always strong and cheerful, that nothing can shake me! They must think I am Superman!

Faiza Al-Araji

TUESDAY, JANUARY 27, 2004

A usual day in my home goes like this. I prepare a breakfast of boiled eggs, white cheese, olives, and some sliced tomatoes and cucumbers, hot tea and bread. Usually I eat breakfast alone because everyone is asleep and I have a lot of work that's waiting to be done so I don't bother anyone and let them sleep late. I then go upstairs to wash clothes; sometimes the electricity is working and sometimes I have to use a generator. By the time the washing is done, the household has risen. Anyway, by the time I've hung the wash to dry on the upper roof or upstairs inside the house, the first part of the day is over. I then hurry to change the family sheets and pillowcases and vacuum the rooms. I rush to the kitchen to wash the breakfast dishes and make lunch.

After lunch, I serve fruit or tea, put up my feet, and take a short rest. If I'm not too tired, I go visit one of the neighbors. By the way, I'm one of those creatures who doesn't like leaving the house unless it's for work, or to go to the store or the doctor. I like to stay at home and I consider that a sign of emotional stability. My joy is here, inside my home, and if I have to search for it elsewhere, then there's something wrong. Even if I'm fighting with Azzam, or one of the boys, I feel the same. It doesn't matter; being alone gives me great joy. I miss that feeling on busy days.

When the kids were young, I used to take them to visit the bird garden or to a small park. Life was more tiring when they were younger, but they were creatures who were easy to handle and used to reply, "Yes mommy, dear?" Now, they are tiring creatures who won't take advice; it bothers them and they think I'm meddling in their business. Sometimes I wish they were small like before, but such thoughts make me smile and I laugh at myself for what passes of our life cannot be brought back.

I remember when I was living in Saudi Arabia I couldn't work. There, women aren't allowed to work, except as teachers, nurses, or doctors. So what was I supposed to do with a degree in civil engineering? Then I found a Saudi architectural bureau, owned by a friend of Azzam, who agreed that I could work on the structural designs for the buildings that the bureau handled, and I could do the work at home.

Professionally, it was a boring experience, but it was financially rewarding. I didn't have any colleagues with whom I could debate work ideas or designs. I used to think in solitude, which was a bothersome process that afforded no fun or professional experience. I had no sense of the days as I spent them trapped in the apartment. Azzam would go to work, dropping Raed off at school. They'd come back at noon and we'd have lunch together. After noon, Azzam would go back to work leaving me, Raed, and Khalid at home together. Khalid still wasn't in school. I would spend the afternoon helping Raed with his homework, playing with Khalid, and then we would watch cartoons together. I couldn't leave the house because in Saudi Arabia a woman is not allowed to go out alone.

In the evenings, Azzam, the kids, and I would go to the supermarket, which I really enjoyed. And of course, I'd have to hide my face with a heavy, thick cloth, and if I attempted to lift it, there would always be someone there to scold me harshly, usually an old man with a long stick that he used to hit people.

We'd spend the weekend outside the city, where the roads were good and the areas were lovely. The children would play with their bicycles and other toys they brought along from home. They'd have a good time, after which we'd go home for baths, then dinner, then sleep. I firmly held to a specific system, so that the house would be in order and the kids would learn to respect rules.

Faiza Al-Araji

Hey all, I am in Jordan now! I arrived just last night for a one week vacation. Amman is the city where I spent my childhood. Today I went to my neighborhood and drove down the street that I used to live. I fondly remember those days.

This street has never been as silent as it is now. There were more than 20 kids, boys and girls, playing together all the time. Innocent childhood; now everything has changed.

All the kids have become men and women. Most of them finished their university studies and many left Jordan and went to try their luck in Europe or the States. There are new buildings everywhere, but this place is still special to me. It's the only thing I have in my life that really connects me to the place that I call home.

I have an identity problem, though. I am Palestinian, but I was born in Saudi Arabia, and have lived in Iraq since 1991. So I am not really sure: Where is home?

Khalid Jarrar

WEDNESDAY, JANUARY 28, 2004

For the last few days, I've been feeling pain in my feet when I stand. When I examined my feet, I found a corn on my heel. It might be a result of the long periods I spend standing in the kitchen. Of course, I had to visit the doctor, and that's the thing I always postpone until it becomes absolutely necessary. I contacted the driver that takes me on such excursions. Before the war I'd go by myself in the afternoon for something like this, but now it's different because there's no security.

The driver took me to the doctor and I asked him to look for a safe spot with a guard and to wait for me. I walked on the sidewalk hesitantly and looked at my friend's pharmacy, which was closed. I asked the man in the shop next to hers what time she opened shop. He shook his head, "They don't open!"

I asked him, "Today only? Or everyday?"

He replied, "They never open and I heard they're offering the shop for sale."

It was evening. I had just heard the dusk call for prayer (Athan il Maghrib). I started up the staircase and at first it was almost empty, which was the first time I had seen it that way. Ever since moving to Iraq in 1991, I'd come to this building any time I, or one of the family, were sick. It had a dentist, a skin doctor, and a general physician—all of them friends of my brothers—they graduated together from Baghdad University.

They all specialized in Britain or America and they had both great professional reputations as well as personal reputations with people. They were all university professors, except Dr. Mohammed who was the dean of the Medical College and head of the Doctor's Syndicate. He was the most intelligent of the group and best in his specialty. The building was always crowded with his patients and they'd even lay around on the sidewalk around his office—especially the ones who had come from distant provinces.

His receptionist used to have to pass the patients on to the waiting room of the dentist. They were friends of the doctor and there was no embarrassment in it. Those are typical Iraqi manners: friendship and affection are more important than money, or even competition.

I always found difficulty in getting an appointment, in spite of the fact that the receptionist had come to know me well. I would call her and she'd give me an appointment for the next day or the day after that. There were rare times when I'd get an appointment the same day, but later than usual, at 9:30, before the clinic would close. I'd agree of course, because you can't postpone an illness. I'd later go down to the pharmacy, which would be crowded with Dr. Mohammed's patients and the patients of the other doctors.

Today I found the building nearly empty and the pharmacy closed. There were only a few patients whispering amongst themselves. I entered the skin clinic and the same old receptionist was sitting there. He hadn't changed, with his sad face and broken smile, as if telling a story of his troubles, of which I had heard several times while waiting to see the doctor.

"Why haven't we seen you in so long?" the old man asked.

I faked a smile, "I don't know. I don't like coming to the building after what happened to Dr. Mohammed."

His face turned sorrowful, and he replied, "Yes. God rest his soul."

"I asked him, "When was the incident. July or August? I can't remember."

"In July." He replied. "It was the middle of July, during the evening, and the building was crowded with patients. Two men walked in and one of them told the secretary that his friend was very sick, was having stomach pain and needed to see the doctor immediately. The receptionist went to the doctor asking permission to let them into his office and he accepted. To the amazement of the receptionist and the patients, the fake patient took out a gun and shot Dr. Mohammed in the head. He and his friend then ran downstairs where a car was waiting for them after they finished their mission. They then disappeared."

I asked, "Do they know who attacked him?"

He shook his head. "No one knows."

"Did he die in his clinic?" I asked.

"No, he died in the hospital half an hour later." He answered.

"Does anyone know the reason?" I beseeched him.

"They said he was a Ba'athist!" The old man said sorrowfully. "So what if he's a Ba'athist. He never hurt anyone. He was peaceful and everyone loved him," he muttered, as if to himself.

He stopped talking then so I didn't reply, but to myself I swore that he was indeed a peaceful man loved by many. He was an intelligent, wonderful thinker and we lost him.

"But the person who killed him didn't know," the old man added. "They paid him and told him go and kill the doctor because he is a Ba'athist. What does he know?"

I stood staring at the ground. Really, what does that contracted killer know about what he did?

I continued asking, "And the clinic?"

"His wife put it up for sale. She kept telling him to leave the country, that it's not safe here, but he refused. He kept saying, "I haven't done anything, I haven't hurt anyone. What do I have to fear?"

Our conversation came to an end when the skin doctor arrived. I entered his office and found him sad also. He told me that he had shut down his clinic for three months out of mourning for Dr. Mohammed. He couldn't believe it had happened. It was a cruel blow to everyone who knew him. He went on to ask me what was wrong with me and he prescribed a mix for my corn, giving me directions to another pharmacy.

As I went down the stairs, I saw the door to his clinic closed and the whole floor was empty. I looked at the walls of the staircase and imagined them carrying him, hurrying to the nearest hospital. I ran down the rest of the stairs in horror as I imagined that perhaps his blood still stained the carpeting in his clinic. Who would dare enter it after what happened? I wondered to myself, *how much did they pay the man who killed him?* And how many tears did his patients and students shed? It's almost as if I can see him and his enemy now—on Judgment Day—before God and he will ask him, smiling, "But why did you kill me? Whatever did I do to you?"

As I reached the sidewalk, the place looked gloomy and abandoned. I stared at the locks on the pharmacy once again and at the bags of garbage littering the sidewalk. My feelings of loneliness increased and I wished I hadn't come here. I'll find another skin doctor, I thought to myself.

Faiza Al-Araji

SUNDAY, FEBRUARY 1, 2004

I have a suggestion: For the next election in the U.S. I think that you should let Osama bin Laden be your president. Just go along with me for a moment. What if that happened? First of all, you will save billions of dollars that are spent on national security because the man will be right there in the White House where you can keep an eye on him, or could you? There will be no more wars on terrorism! Wouldn't that be nice? No more dead soldiers. No more money spent on wars. No more tragedy. Isn't that what we all want?

Plus, Bush would be really pissed off. That alone would be worth it.

Khalid Jarrar

FRIDAY, FEBRUARY 6, 2004

I am still in Amman. Khalid and Majed returned to Baghdad to follow up on school matters, as studies haven't started yet. Raed stayed with me; today is his birthday. We are having a small party for him at his aunt's house. All of his little cousins will be there.

I went out to do some shopping. I bought a birthday gift and a strawberry and whipping cream cake for Raed. It looks so delicious. When I got home, I found that Raed had a guest. He is an American working for a news medium that is against the war on Iraq. He has been in Amman for two days and is trying to go to Baghdad to write about American companies and the truth of their activities in Iraq. He doesn't speak Arabic and he has money, so he is afraid that it will get stolen. Raed agreed to keep some of his money here and we would give it to him in Baghdad. Raed helped him to get a reservation with a group of Iraqis in a car heading to Baghdad. That is better than him traveling on his own. He will travel in the evening.

I always wonder when I meet a foreigner, *is he afraid of us?* Does he think we will betray him or hurt him? We usually have sympathy with such people, we take care of them and we surround them with care until they get back to their family. When one of the foreigners that we know through various organizations gets hurt, we all hurry to give him support. Not because we are agents to America, but because it is a humanitarian issue. We say this person is not responsible for what happened. Just like us; we are not responsible either. I was asked a question by a group of young women writing a report about the war in Iraq. How do you see the American families involved in the war in your country? I see them as victims just like us. They are paying the price for a bill due to the big investors that will earn lots of money from this. We are the losers. We, the people. I don't look at it the way bin Laden does. "The base of the government is a nation that is supporting war and oppression." That is why he is resorting to violence and murder towards the base. I see this vision as being stupid, hostile, and unrealistic. For example the Vietnam war stopped as a result of pressure on the government from average people. We hoped the same would happen with regards to the war on Iraq. That means that our help and support is the American people.

The American people are not our enemy and we shouldn't direct murder or violence against them. Even those that are sympathetic to us have a different vision than we do. We have a saying, *The people of Mecca are more knowledgeable about its pathways.* That means that those that are dedicated, nationalistic, and loyal to Iraq have an independent vision that is suitable for their country. These people know the history of their country. That aids them is creating a leadership by the people that would execute a beneficial program. From all our pains we no longer trust political parties. Only God knows who is funding and directing them.

We want a dignified and free life. We want a life with justice and guaranteed human rights for each citizen. And freedom. A freedom that is respectful and doesn't hurt others. We don't need imported ideas and strange experiments. You can't grow strawberries in the desert. These need a suitable climate to grow and flourish. Where is the suitable context for a Western democracy? Each place has its own context. We should respect those and give them ample consideration, otherwise we turn out to be fools. We either become a target for criticism from a peaceful opposition or we become ripe for violence and murder from an opposition that has a different value system. This will only leave more victims and more complicated issues with no solutions on the horizon.

Faiza Al-Araji

WEDNESDAY, FEBRUARY 11, 2004

I am still in Amman. I am leaving tomorrow evening with Raed for Baghdad. I have missed Baghdad so much. There was a small earthquake in Amman this morning. Schools and buildings were evacuated, and people were standing out in the streets. This caused stifling traffic jams; I could hardly find a taxi.

Today I got many e-mails; most of them from America. They were critical of one of my previous articles in which I mentioned that Capitalism is a bad idea. Everybody is upset at me; they felt I was being unfair toward Capitalism. I would like to clarify my point. I think that capitalism is useful to a society because everybody gets the chance to live his life and fulfill his ambitions. But we have seen nothing except the ugly side of capitalism: Military occupation and looting.

In our country, we try to emulate the West, but the companies that start up find no competition and control the market. Over here survival is not of the fittest, but of the cruelest. This reflects on people's manners and the way they treat each other. Money becomes the priority. All the sincere relationships between people become tainted. We are a nation that is used to giving first priority to values and ideals, not materialism. All this confusion is making us pour our anger at the Western Capitalist system, where religion and state are separated. Religion is a private matter; nobody should interfere with it. Religion is a beautiful value that teaches us boundaries. Religion prevents us from committing foolish acts that destroy our lives and the lives of others. We don't steal, we don't kill, we don't oppress other people, we don't bribe, and we don't destroy our family life with relationships that are not innocent. That leads us to respect ourselves and find the sacred things in life that give us respect.

Many people in Western societies are returning to religion. But how many, and what influence do they have? Perhaps their numbers are few because their ability to influence decision making is limited. Governments over there don't make decisions from a religious point of view. Had they been religious they would have not resorted to wars against other nations. In reality the reasons for the war were purely economic: To find new markets and find new sources of wealth and to revive a failing economy. And as for the role of the individual: Should he stay quiet and complacent with his government, since he will benefit from all these efforts, for himself and his children's future, even if it destroys the lives of others? I don't believe in violence as a way to solve problems. I believe in opening civilizations to each other and living in peace.

An Arabic proverb says that people are the enemies of that which they are ignorant. This ignorance in the relationship between us and the West, which makes us hate each other; we believe all the accusations made against the other party. It is a defense mechanism to protect our beliefs; people do that when their understanding of the world is limited. If I don't understand someone, then it is easy for me to take an extreme stance against that person. I might justify his killing or his destruction because I don't think that he deserves to live like I do. Because I hold values that I believe in and I am distrustful of other values. Why give him a chance? He is nothing—let him go to hell. Isn't that true of how the West views Muslims? And the way Muslims view the West? Each side thinks that they are right and the other side is wrong; the other wants to interfere with my life. I won't give him the chance, let him go to hell. When I was little, even as a young woman, I used to hear that the West had no values, their families were broken, their relationships were bad, they had AIDS, perverts, prostitutes, and drunks. When I began meeting Westerners, especially after this last war, I met many who were smart and well-mannered. I found that they are people just like us. They have families and values. Who distorted their image in our minds like that? And then I ask myself, how do they see us? Maybe they see us as an ignorant and stupid bunch? Maybe they think we all ride camels, are all terrorists like bin Laden. We don't understand anything except violence. Our cultures need to open up one to another, so that we can see properly from all angles. I remember a Qur'anic verse, "We created you different nations and tribes so that you would know one another, the most righteous are those that fear God the most." That means the most just, the most close to God without a nationalistic identity. There are no special privileges with God. I feel like there is some kind of a mistake in the way we see each other. This mistake was caused by the barrier between us; barriers of language and culture. We must on both sides attempt to destroy these barriers and create a closeness and understanding, so that the next generations can live in a beautiful world in peace. A world that is better than the one our generation lives in, without useless wars and destruction.

Faiza Al-Araji

SATURDAY, FEBRUARY 14, 2004

At last! I am back in Baghdad. It is now four o'clock in the afternoon. The electricity went out, so we turned on the electric generator. Now that I have returned to the routine of my daily life I feel completely relaxed.

The road from Amman to Baghdad goes through mostly desert. We reached the Jordanian border at six in the morning. We gave them our passports and waited along with about 50 others; some Jordanians, a few foreigners, and many Iraqis. There were very few people working the border and they worked slowly. So to pass the time I went outside to get some fresh air and get away from the screaming kids, the crowds, and the cigarette smoke. I found many parked cars; women and children were sleeping in them. I felt sorry for them. I saw an employee wearing the official uniform of a border officer. So I said good morning to him and he responded with a polite smile. I told him that there are lots of people waiting and the work is proceeding too slowly. We have been waiting for an hour and a half and haven't received our passports back. He told me that he didn't work there, but that he worked with customs. I went back into the waiting room. I have a feeling he won't do anything but it made me feel better to complain to somebody. I sat down and looked around the place. The floor was covered with cigarette butts and empty, plastic coffee cups. Many of the chairs were broken. The walls are dirty and the air conditioner had a thick layer of dirt on it.

When the American forces entered Iraq, we used to talk about all the things we would do and how we would behave. I would always say, and I still do today, that the occupation will end sooner or later. I was hoping to learn good things from the occupation, like respect for people, the value of a human life, the government preserving the rights of an individual, the right to vote for whom you see fit, and the benefits of new technologies. I mean, this is what Westerners stand for, so why don't we learn from it?

When I reached the first Iraqi checkpoint, two hours from Baghdad, the place was filthy; plastic bags and empty cartons and tin cans littered the floor. I would feel embarrassed if I was bringing over a foreigner with me from abroad. What would I tell him? I don't know. I have no answer. When visitors come to our land from other countries, we prefer to show them that our country is beautiful and that we are intelligent humans with dreams just like them.

I remember visiting one of my relatives when I was little. I was surprised by how clean her house was. It was full of toys that she made herself. She had a degree in fine arts. She would also sew the school uniforms. Unfortunately, my father couldn't afford to make us any other clothes except school clothes. I used to love visiting her house. I would dream that when I grew up and got married I would have a beautiful home like hers. My children would be always be clean like her children.

When I got married and left Iraq for many years. After I returned, my mom reminded me of her. She told me to go visit her but she warned me that her situation has changed. During the Irani war, the government terminated services for everyone of Persian origin. They were all forced to retire with small pensions that were barely enough to survive on. She was the principle of the school and her husband was a government employee. They both lost their positions suddenly. It was torture to find try to find her new address in neighborhood she was living in. When I found her she greeted me with the same good-natured smile and soft-spoken style. But a part of my heart was breaking as I looked around the house. The furniture was cheap and old, as were the curtains; the house was a mess; nothing was organized or beautiful as I remembered it to be. An ugly picture without a frame hung on the wall. I couldn't believe it! Are these the same people that I remembered so vividly? I asked her how they survive. She told me that they took a part of the house and turned it into a small store that her husband runs. She told me that it helps them survive. She showed me the store. It was a depressing room with metal shelves covered with more dust than merchandise.

Why did I remember this woman as I crossed the border? Maybe because the neglect and chaos that I saw there is similar to this. I think that is the cause for the destruction of human life. We lose meaning in our lives; the beauty and zest for life is now gone. We are a depressed nation. We harbored big dreams, but they were destroyed one way or the other. Our dreams of freedom, independence, truth in dealing with one another. Who destroyed it? Who turned our private and public lives into a hurricane of chaos and confusion? Was it destroyed by four consecutive centuries of Ottoman colonization? Was it damaged by the British colonization that lasted half a century? Or was it foreign governments? I wish I knew.

At the Iraqi border the processing was light. There was a single person and he was stamping the passports without paying much attention to what he was doing. I don't know how to explain this. Is the neglect due to the fact that there is no state in power? There were a few American soldiers, but they kept their distance from the border. The sight of them breaks my heart because it reminds me of the disaster of the military occupation. Hours before we traveled, I was saying goodbye to my sister and her husband. They had guests from Baghdad. I encouraged staying in Baghdad despite all the dangers. If we all decide to leave, then who will stay behind? Who will I leave Iraq to? I decided that I would stay in Iraq. If I can live to see a democratic Iraq that we create according to our beliefs, then I will be happy because I had participated in a small way. If I die then I will be happy because I died here in my country. My sister and her husband laughed at me. Yes, perhaps I am a bit naïve. But I still dream about my homeland, truth, justice, and freedom. I believe in that just like I believe in God; just like I believe in His existence and His divine justice; just like I believe that God is with the truth and with those that seek it. How can I choose a life far away with a clear head? I could stay here and bare the difficulty of these cruel days. Hopefully, we will see the light that will appear at the end of the darkness; after the end of the chaos, murders, and destruction that is taking place in Iraq. I wonder, will I be one of those that is lucky enough to see the Iraq we have dreamt of? Or will I be just another name on the list of victims who died?

Faiza Al-Araji

THURSDAY, FEBRUARY 15, 2004

Yesterday was Valentine's Day. While the rest of the world was being inundated with love letters, flowers, and gifts, Iraq was inundated with the horrors of war. I got e-mails consoling me and blaming Bush for everything that has happened. I also got angry e-mails making excuses and defending him, but I can read between the lines. What they were really saying is that Iraqis are ungrateful for the sacrifices made the Bush administration.

Who can believe that a Capitalist system, which thinks in terms of loss and profit, has suddenly turned into some charitable organization that wages wars against evil and freely sacrifices its money and the lives of its youth to bring justice and freedom to another country, tens of thousands of kilometers away, that doesn't share its ideologies or culture? Bush makes me sad when he says that he wishes he could put a fence around America and not deal with any other country in the world because they don't understand or appreciate America's sacrifices for them. And if he did, then people all over the world would start screaming, "Where are you, America; why don't you come to save us?'"

All of you who live in America have a government that ensures your rights, but at the same time interferes in the business of other countries and humiliates the people there, and trivializes their history and culture. The Bush administration wants Iraqis to shed our identities and submit to it. The Bush administration wants us to live life the way it sees fit, with no arguments and no objections.

The Bush administration was planning this war for many years and it started the war without heeding the warnings that other countries issued, especially the West European countries. But the Bush administration was stubborn and so sure of itself that it wouldn't give in to pressure, and it announced its rage at such warnings and acted with hostility towards Germany, France, and Russia. The Bush administration beat the drums of war and the regime fell and an occupation was imposed. Bush gave speeches and declared victory while his supporters stood by and applauded. We were watching our television screens wondering, *Do we applaud Bush, too, or weep for our country?*

An intimidating army attacked a country that was just barely breathing and they enjoy victory and applause? It's the equivalent of a downcast, a failure of a man who owns a tractor and wants to convince himself he's a hero, so he attacks a faraway hut and destroys it around the family inside, simply to get applause from the passersby in the street. He's not the only idiot; the applauders are like him, and have the same principles and values. The strong eat the weak; this is the law of the jungle.

But the catastrophes then befell the Bush administration, with murders and looting in the streets of Iraq. Explosions targeting the American army and the confused Iraqis wondering, *What is happening*? Either this was a badly planned war by a corrupt administration or everything was done on purpose with the intent of causing more damage until Iraq collapses, and its people and treasures are taken unawares. If the first possibility is correct, then Bush should resign because he failed the mission he had taken upon himself to build a new, strong, free country. If the second possibility is correct, then Bush is once more the loser because he has started a whirlpool of violence that has no end.

At the beginning of the fall of Baghdad, we were optimistic; we said we'll give them a chance and not think badly of them. As time passed, and all of the reasons for the invasion were proved wrong, we could no longer accept the idea of their innocence no matter what happened. It is as if all the Bush administration wants to do is cause strife between the Sunnis and the Shi'ites and the Arabs and the Kurds. In whose best interest is it to break apart the Iraqi police and push for a longer occupation?

The Bush administration is confused; after waving the banner of war by itself, it now comes up with a new motto: The whole world should work together to create peace. It began searching for troops from all over the world to replace its own troops, who were heading back home. What was the point of years of planning if the results were going to be as catastrophic as this? Of course, the capture of Saddam was a winning card for Bush, as it improved his popularity.

But the Iraqis say the American government will not want a trial for Saddam. A trial will expose certain secrets that America doesn't want the world to hear. Saddam was America's ally, and then they turned against him, or he turned against them. It doesn't really matter; the results are the same. As an old proverb goes, Imperialism doesn't have any friends. Saddam Hussein chose his friends badly and he didn't think they'd sell him so cheaply and abandon him so easily.

And the projects that the Iraqis are waiting for—the ones that will invigorate the economy and create jobs—where are they? We hear about some of them being given to foreign companies for huge sums of money and some to local contractors, also at very high prices, and people laugh and whisper that the American official wants his piece of the contract before signing it. Where is the American public? I wish they could see and hear what is happening here! The average American citizen all the way over there thinks they've sent angels as representatives to uphold justice on earth. The reality of the situation is very different.

Mobile phones have arrived in Baghdad, but no one can afford them because one company got the whole contract for Baghdad without any competition. This company sets whatever prices it likes and forces the consumer to buy the phone with the line; you cannot just subscribe to the line if you already have a phone. Who gave this contract to this company? And why did they give it the right to control the whole market? What is the point of the Americans? And how involved are they in helping? Furthermore, is a deal like this considered transparent and far from suspicion?

Next month, a year will have passed since the beginning of the war, and the month after will a mark a year since the end of the war. What has been done? Everything is moving so slowly, and time is wasting away as we wait. The American media is convincing the people that everything here is okay. All the while, we see insufficiency in everything and we don't know if it's on purpose or accidental, but the performance so far is weak and far less than we expected. America will never stop intruding in the business of other countries, from military affairs to the economy, from the media to education.

The governments that follow America's directions are thrown a few crumbs to improve the economy and keep that government in power. The internal affairs of that government don't matter; neither does the relationship between the government and its people. The important thing is to satisfy America—that is the main thing that will ensure survival.

Governments that don't follow the directions face the drums of war in the media and files are opened either about nuclear weapons or human rights! Aren't these stories old? Who are they fooling? Their people or ours? And I think back to the idea that America would put a fence around itself. It's a wonderful idea. I smile to myself and imagine what the world would be like without Big

Brother watching to make sure you follow his directions. I think it would be a happier world than this one.

Faiza Al-Araji

WEDNESDAY, FEBRUARY 25, 2004

These days the electricity is coming on fairly regularly: On for three hours, off for three hours. We are used to it now and we no longer complain about it. We moved into this house nine years ago. Raed was finishing up high school, Khalid was in primary school, and Majed was just a kid. Now, Raed graduated from university a few years ago, Khalid is in college, and Majed will finish high school this summer and will go to university next year. I remember those days with a smile. These days I sometimes wake up in the middle of the night and it is quiet, calm, and dark, except for the sounds of tanks driving down the road, rumbling in the distance and getting closer. That is when I can hear the sound of metal knocking and shaking, so I hide under my bed covers.

I think about Iraqi children; what have they seen in their short lives? Especially those that were born in the nineties; they were raised on bombs and cannons, instead of toys and fun. Their vocabulary consists of war, Saddam, and Bush. During the war with Iraq, it was Bush the father; in this war it is Bush the son. It is as if these two had some sort of a family feud to settle with Iraq. The son is here to finish his father's war. When Clinton was in power we didn't hear much from him, even though he remembered us with a few rockets. But he wasn't as hostile towards us as the Bushes. I don't know, perhaps there is some great secret pushing them to punish Iraq. I am afraid of the consequences if Bush doesn't win the next election. The power in the U.S. is in the hands of the wealthy who like to direct things according to their interests, so they may very well limit the power of a new president who may want to end the war. We and the American public will be the losers.

Faiza Al-Araji

THURSDAY, FEBRUARY 26, 2004

Azzam is away on a trip. Work has become exhausting for me. I am forced to stay longer hours at work and I get home late. I spend my time answering the customers' questions about various orders for pumps, drinking water systems, and lab equipment. It is easy to deal with orders when the equipment is already available, but when we don't have it at the store I have to go back to the catalogs, look up prices, and submit proposals, technical specifications, and delivery time to Baghdad. All these details give me a headache.

I enjoy reading the long e-mails that people send me, the ones that read like novels. They are like bridges of love and trust between Iraq and the rest of the world. Most of the e-mails I got this week were positive and made me happy. I got e-mails from the U.S., Canada, and Europe. Many of them are mothers my own age; their memories are genuine and beautiful. They make me smile and make me feel that the distances between us are getting shorter. I feel that we can understand each others' perspective. One letter in particular made me happy and surprised me at the same time; it was a letter from an American soldier on his way to serve in Iraq. He asked my permission to call me ma'am. He said that he loves Iraq and that he wants to help out. He said that he learned from his Muslim superior how to behave in a Muslim country, and how to be respectful of other people's feelings because he truly wants to help. He told me that he was against the war and is sorry about the suffering of the Iraqi people. He wishes us freedom and peaceful lives. I sent him a reply, in which I thanked him and asked him not to hesitate to call me when he gets to Baghdad, especially if he needs any help. He replied by saying that it would be against Army regulations for him to do so.

Another American sent me excerpts from Hammurabi's law in his e-mail. This is the oldest law in human civilization. His e-mail was very respectful toward the nation of Iraq. He says that the American people love peace but the government only thinks about the type of peace that is in accordance with its self interest.

The Iraqis and the Americans are thinking: What does the other side want? What is their perspective? The Iraqi Web sites contain writing that is representative of a small part of our society. And the e-mails that we get are representative of a small part of their society. These are bridges that help us build ties of trust and respect between our two nations. A small percentage of the e-mails I receive from Americans are hostile. I usually delete those right after I read them; I believe that the people who write these hostile messages do not have the capacity to think clearly. When the issue of the Iraqi occupation becomes a point of contention among the American people as they are about to enter presidential elections, it is a positive thing. This occupation has been a disaster for all of us, but I am sure that is has made the American public reevaluate things. It has made people think about the usefulness of the military presence here. They are becoming convinced that Iraq is not a threat to them. Maybe they will start thinking that Iraq needs their help and support to build a new country that is suitable to its people, religion, and values. A foreign hand will ruin and distort our values and our religion, intentionally or unintentionally. The American people should pressure their current and upcoming governments to get started on the reconstruction plans for Iraq; and the reconstruction should be done in a truthful and transparent manner, like they do in America, and subjected to accounting and questioning. While Iraq is in a state of chaos, there is no room for accounting and questioning. The responsibly will remain with the occupation forces. I hope that they appreciate this situation and treat it in a serious and just manner. If this doesn't happen, then it will reflect badly on the Americans.

Yesterday I had to go to work in the evening, and on my way home, there was an American security checkpoint on the street leading to our house. When my turn came, the American soldier walked up to my car and directed a light at me. The street was dark, so I opened the window. He directed me to go to another checkpoint on another street where my car would be searched. I told him that my house is on this street; if I go to the other street I will be going away from my home. I didn't want to be late getting home, so I asked if he could just search my car here, but he said very angrily, "No! Go there," as he pointed with his hand in the direction of the other checkpoint

I said, "But I am a woman, I don't want to be late. Don't you care?"

He said that it didn't matter to him, so I raised my voice and told him he should care. Then I turned and went to the other checkpoint, where I had to wait my turn again. Then the same soldier walked to my car again with the light in his hand. He whispered that he hoped I wasn't annoyed; I told him that I was. He told me he was sorry, but that he was following orders. I smiled and felt sorry for him. I wondered who brought this poor guy over here and made him confront me like this. He is afraid of me and I am afraid of him. He is suspicious of me and I am suspicious of him. When I got to the other checkpoint, there was an Iraqi accompanying several American soldiers. He smiled and apologized and asked me to open the trunk and they searched the car. I wished them a good evening and went back home. I felt more sorrow than anger. I wished they would all return safely to their families.

Faiza Al-Araji

FRIDAY, FEBRUARY 27, 2004

Today is the weekend, when the whole family gets together and we have breakfast and lunch together. This doesn't always happen during the week since our schedules are so different with school and work. On the weekend I always cook something special, since I have lots of time. Today I cooked stuffed vegetables called dolma, which includes zucchini, cucumber, and peppers. You can also add onions and other vegetables but I wanted to keep it simple.

The woman that helps me clean the house came today with her son, who is younger than Majed. They are a poor, well mannered, and trustworthy family. She has lots of dignity, which I really like about her; I respect her greatly for it. I would never have anyone but her clean my home. I finished cooking and she cleaned up afterward. I served lunch for myself and the kids in the kitchen and for her and her son in the garden where the sun was shining. I don't like to eat while they wait; I believe that would be insulting to them and in bad taste on my part.

I remember the words of the prophet Muhammad (peace be upon him) when referring to poor people: "Feed them from what you eat and dress them from your own clothes." I usually donate some of my clothes and shoes that are in good shape. I am too ashamed to give away something that is not clean and ironed. I feel it might insult the person who receives it. I like to be generous and treat people as I would like to be treated.

Friday is a day of prayer for Muslims. People go to mosques and other places of worship. Khalid and Majed decided to go out for prayers. I was worried about them with all the explosions that are happening all over, but they got home safely. Each time they go somewhere, I stay worried and I recite verses from the Qur'an in my heart. I keep praying to God that they return home safely. I think that belief in God is a person's last resort in time of hardship.

This is the first month of the higri year (Muslim calendar). We use the regular Western calendar for our daily life, business dealings, and birthdays. I don't know at what point we stopped using the Islamic calendar as the official calendar in Arabic countries. I know people are more committed to the Muslim calendar in Persian gulf countries like Saudi Arabia; it has remained symbolic in most Arabic countries.

The first ten days of this month commemorate the killing of Hussein, may peace be upon him. He was the son of Fatima, the youngest daughter of the prophet Muhammad. Hussein attempted a now famous revolution against the Ummayed ruling family at the time, when there was lots of corruption and oppression in the ruling ranks. People in Iraq pleaded with Hussein, who was then living in the Arabian peninsula. Hussein decided to answer the call and traveled to Iraq with his family, brothers, their wives, and children;

about 70 people in all. Negotiations took place between them and the ruler in Syria, who threatened them. Messengers were sent to warn Hussein from entering into a battle because he would lose. They told him that the people of Iraq are with him in heart, but their swords would be used against him.

History books mention that he considered withdrawing and returning to his home. He wasn't interested in power and wealth; rather, he was an honorable person wanting to support the poor and weak and stand up to the corrupt rulers. According to history books, the oppressive ruler wouldn't allow Hussein to return home. He was afraid that the opposition would strengthen and he would come back to fight him at a later point. So he sent an army to surround them. On the tenth day of Muharam, close to a water well in Karbala, they were denied access to water and they were killed. Hussein and his supporters fought honorably, but all were killed.

As for the women and children, they were taken as prisoners to Syria, along with the severed head of Hussein to show to the ruler. Hussein's revolution remained alive in stories that people tell from one generation to the next, about an honorable man who wouldn't stay silent in the face of oppression. He paid the price with his life and the life of his family.

Now everywhere you look in Baghdad you see black flags, in memory of the death of Hussein. Many households cook and donate food to the poor. When we cook on this occasion, we stir the food in the pot with a huge spatula while saying, "May peace be upon you, O! father of Abed Allah, may God have mercy on you, God bless you and bless your place in heaven with the martyrs and prophets." I love this story, but it is so painful. I don't like the exaggerations in the story, like hitting oneself on the head or the self-whipping.

These are violent and hurtful acts that bare no relation to the story of Hussein. Remembering the story of Hussein brings up noble, refined, and beautiful values that are inspiring to the soul. They make a person remember the values that Hussein died for, the very values that are about to become extinct. We now live in a time where people are willing to die for material things.

Faiza Al-Araji

SATURDAY, FEBRUARY 28, 2004

I surfed the Internet and checked my e-mail. There were e-mails I read that made me smile, and one e-mail in which the writer asked me to teach him the Arabic words for greeting and welcoming. He wasn't the first to ask for this help. There was a previous letter from Portugal whose sender asked for the address of a site that taught Arabic. Another person from Australia said that he wanted to learn Arabic so that he could read the blogs before they were translated. All those letters made me happy and gave me the impression that people like our language and are eager to learn something about it, even if only simple words like: marhaba, shukran, and ma'a il salama. This creates affection between people and supports the theory that the world has become a small village.

I went to the butcher to buy some chopped and minced meat. Azzam usually does this but he is traveling. The man said, "Please have a seat—you'll have to wait a quarter of an hour while I finish up my work." I had no choice but to sit and wait because our freezer was empty and I needed to buy something. As the man started working, I bided my time looking out on the street.

A group of children entered the shop accompanied by an old lady in an abbaya [black cloak-like garb]. She said to the small girl, "Come in, dear, this is the 'shams il baqila' [horse bean sun]. Don't sit too long in it, you'll catch typhoid." An identical phrase came to mind: My mother (God have mercy upon her soul) used to say the same thing to me when I was a little girl, sitting on the roof sunning myself and reading. 'Shams il baqila' [horse bean sun]. As I grew older, I understood. This is a particularly hot sun that speeds the growth of horse beans in the winter (even though the beans love the heat), and they are available for most of the summer. In the winter though, they

121

are available only for a short period and are often expensive, then they disappear to return again in the summer.

I smiled and looked at the little ones—three girls and a boy. They approached the butcher and the little one yanked on his pants and shouted, "Give me some money. I want chocolate!" The butcher laughed and opened the drawer, handing out paper money. I imagined parents on Eid Day, handing out 'Eidiyat' [gifts of money] to the little children with their voices raised in shouts and mirth. The kids ran out of the store to the neighboring shop.

I finished purchasing the meat, fruit, and cheeses from different stores on the same sidewalk. Before I entered the car, I glanced at my watch and noted that it was two in the afternoon. I noticed an Iraqi police car standing at the beginning of the street I'm accustomed to taking home every day, so I took another street. Everything looked normal until I got to a point on the road leading to the airport where there was a sizeable crowd that spread well into the horizon. I began slowing the car. There were dozens of small cars and trucks blowing their horns, large buses, and the smell of smoke. I looked at the car windows of the small cars around me and their passengers. I looked at my watch—it was almost three—I should have been home over half an hour ago, and here I was just starting the trip home! I took out the mobile phone and called the kids. "Where are you mom?" I heard them yelling. "I'm stuck on the airport road. There's a traffic jam, some sort of a problem. Don't worry about me."

The cars were moving very slowly. Helicopters flew above us and hovered low, then went far away, as if there was some battlefield nearby. I turned and opened the bags. I made myself a small kebab sandwich and opened a can of soda. I decided I would ignore everything that was happening and enjoy my time. I turned on the radio to listen to some music.

A truck full of American soldiers passed on my left; in front of it and behind it were Humvees. I watched them from behind the glass. On normal days, they would pass quickly, but today, they were stuck in the traffic as well.

There was something strange in the middle of the truck. The soldiers were sitting to the left and to the right with their guns aimed and there was something in the middle I couldn't identify at first. It moved and I thought it was some sort of an animal. I couldn't believe it—an animal? What would the troops be doing with an animal? I continued driving my car slowly with my gaze stuck on the truck. In a moment, I realized that the strange creature was actually a human. A human sitting on his knees with his hands tied behind his back and a rough sack on his head. I wondered what this person could have done. Did he throw a bomb at them or simply get in their way?

I thought of the possible destination of this person. Would he disappear for months in their detainee camps for questioning? These idiotic policies are creating an air of animosity against the American presence, and the people can't be blamed. If that man with the bag on his head had been surrounded by Iraqi police, I would have felt sympathetic to his situation. But when American troops surround an Iraqi civilian it's a provocative sight and one word jumps to mind: occupation. And you feel anger and insult.

The crowd lessened for a moment and the American car sped off in the direction of the airport and we all went off in another direction as the Iraqi guards shouted, "Take any other direction except the airport—they'll shoot at you!" I don't know. There was also an attack against them near the airport.

I started on the trip home, and got there around four o'clock, almost two hours late. Thank God, I said to myself, that I didn't get hit with a stray bullet. I have learned to look at the bright side of things. I knocked on the door and heard the sound of the kids welcoming me home.

Faiza Al-Araji

SUNDAY, FEBRUARY 29, 2004

Today was a hectic day at work. I took care of many customers that were working with humanitarian organizations. I respect them very much because they are risking their lives for others. These people remind me that good hasn't been cut away from all humans: there are still those who believe in helping humanity.

Then one of my relatives called and her voice just didn't sound right to me. I asked her what was wrong and she told me that her son had been abducted this morning while he was on his way to the university. People dragged him out of the car and took him away. He called from his mobile phone and told his father that he was in the trunk of the car. "I've been kidnapped by someone," he said.

We hear these stories every day and I expect it to happen to me or my kids. No one has protection. We leave our homes terrified and return the same way. Those relatives of ours own a shop and they have new cars. Those are the two things that attract thieves— especially since they don't live in an expensive neighborhood. I called the boys to tell them I was going to be late, and went directly to our relative's house. I got to the parking area of their building and parked my car. I calmly stepped out and knocked on the door. One of the guests opened it. The house was strangely silent, though full of people.

I said, "Al Salamu Alaikum. God willing he'll be back safe." I wasn't sure what to say to someone on an occasion like this. The father thanked me and told me to go inside where the women were. He pointed to the right and I went to the room where the boy's mother, her relatives, and neighbors were sitting. She was pale and her eyes were swollen. I held her to me and said, "Be patient and pray to God that he may be back safe." I sat and listened to her telling the story.

"I told him in the morning, 'Don't take the car—I need it today.' " She said. "But he was stubborn and he went off to college. His father had left for work before him, but he came back early and told me that our son had called him and said that some unknown people had abducted him. He was in the trunk of the car and they were taking him to a strange place." He had left the car near the house. The car, of course, had been an old model and that was probably why they didn't take it. Had it been one of those newer cars, they would have taken it with the boy. And now we were sitting and waiting for them to call and give their conditions.

There is no ideal way to prevent such things from happening. If the boy leaves alone in his car, they'll abduct him. If he leaves with a driver—related or not—no one can prevent an abduction. We heard of many situations. Every story has different details that leads one to believe that there is no way to prevent it. There are even people who were abducted from right in the middle of their personal bodyguards, so I know it's not from a lack of caution.

I am convinced that it is a case of God's will—he does what he wants. I recalled a short story Tolstoy had written about a man sleeping in the forest. A bee came along to sting him; it hovered and hovered and an angel chased it away. A bear came along—or something like that, I can't remember exactly—but couldn't hurt the man. Then came thieves who wanted to steal his wallet, and somehow they ended up running away without taking it. Several tragedies occurred, but not a single one harmed him. He woke up, smiled, yawned, and said, "What a lovely place this is. And how safe it is!" Of course, he didn't know there was an angel guarding him, smiling, and standing by his side. I still believe in that angel, or I wouldn't be here, and I wouldn't be able to cope with the daily difficulties.

I got home before dark. I called my relatives late at night. There had been a phone call from the abductors and negotiations. They told them that they would call in the morning to give them the final answer. How will the night pass for his mother, father, and siblings? I stayed up thinking all night and waiting for morning.

Faiza Al-Araji

TUESDAY, MARCH 2, 2004

Today is Ashoura holiday. We decided to stay indoors; the kids slept in. I cooked food for Ashoura, like I do every year. I divided the food into small pots so that I could give it away. My sister called me this morning to tell me that there were explosions. This ruined my mood. For some time now, I try not to answer the phone, because I am afraid of hearing bad news like this. But there is no escaping reality; the news will get to me, one way or the other. I stayed worried all day long, thinking about all the people that I know that usually go visit the shrines and mosques in Baghdad and Karbala on this day. In the evening I found e-mails from many concerned friends asking about us and expressing their sorrow over these events. I also spend a fair bit of time answering the e-mails so they won't worry.

Mr. Bremer said in the evening that the coalition forces will enforce tight inspections at the borders. I said thank you. Finally they remembered that the borders are a weak spot that is used by criminals. But the coalition forces have their own priorities. To secure safe conditions for themselves. At the end of the list comes the Iraqi nation. This is how we lived with Saddam, and this is how we live today.

Members of the Governing Council are complaining that the coalition forces are controlling security, the economy, and the media. We, the people, smile and ask, "So what is left for the Governing Council?" Security. That is the first priority for Iraqis, then the economy; let the media go to hell. We want the coalition forces to provide these two so that it will be the start of a trusting relationship between them and the Iraqis. When will this become the first priority? We are waiting.

Faiza Al-Araji

WEDNESDAY, MARCH 3, 2004

I hear there is a draft version of the constitution, and that it will be final soon. I don't like this new constitution, because it reinforces the division among Iraqi people based on ethnic origin. Iraq has become divided into Shia, Sunni, Arab, Turkmen, and Kurdish. This was not the case in the past. This is not the way to unite a nation; this is a way to divide people. I get e-mails from all over the world asking me if I am Sunni or Shia. You can hear people saying Sunni, Shia, Sunni, Shia; what a disaster. What is the difference between Sunni and Shia? They are all Muslims. Instead of looking for the things that unite us so that we can become one nation under these difficult conditions, we have become a nation divided into tribes and ethnic groups. Is this the right way to build the new Iraq?

When a customer comes to the store saying, "We the Shia should get our turn now because we are the majority" (by *we* he means him and me), I feel embarrassed and I look around. I think about how this talk is confrontational to the Sunni standing next to me. This kind of talk is inappropriate. I hate this sense of divisiveness. We are one nation with equal rights; that is what I believe in. Some small minded people become happy when they hear such talk. I feel sorry for such people. I feel that a person like this is misguided, and he will waste many years of his life only to discover that he has taken the wrong path.

We used to employ a Kurdish engineer at our store. He worked with us for many years fixing electronic devices. Azzam and I would treat him with respect and compassion. We would invite him over to our house for lunch and for coffee and tea. Then he got married and had a family. He asked for a salary raise. We didn't hesitate. We tried to treat him exceptionally because he was Kurdish, and the Kurds are an oppressed minority group. We would give him extra attention. We tried to compensate for any feeling of alienation he may experience in our society. When the war began we had to close down the store until the security situation calmed down a bit. Then we reopened the store and returned to work. I felt that we needed him back; many customers required repairs on their equipment. So I sent somebody to his house to tell him. After a while he came into the store. We sat to drink coffee, and we asked him about the war and how he got through those difficult days. We talked about the destruction that happened to the city. As we were talking we mentioned the political parties that seized the houses of government officials, clubs, and governmental offices and tried to turn them into their headquarters.

We criticized such behavior. These are buildings belonging to the state; they shouldn't be abused by a particular party. We mentioned examples, this political party, that political party, and then we mentioned a Kurdish party. Suddenly he became agitated and jumped angrily out of his chair. What is wrong with Kurdish parties? He started to yell and got angry. He said how Kurdish people were oppressed under the Saddam regime and the Arabs did nothing about it. The time has come for Kurdish people to be free and do as they will. I couldn't believe that this hostile person was also the peaceful man that used to work for us; the same person that was shy and always had a smile on his face. It caused me lots of pain to see him like that. I feel sorry for what is happening to him. The smell of hateful racism was coming out of him.

I raised my voice and told him, "You have worked with us for many years. Did we once mistreat you? Did we once not pay you on time because you are Kurdish? Have we ever disrespected you because you are Kurdish? Haven't you discovered that Saddam oppressed us all; he didn't spare anybody. I am Shia, but do I hate Sunnis because they were close to Saddam? That would be stupid. Saddam was close to anybody who was willing to act like a hypocrite." He didn't answer my questions. He left the store. I don't know if it was out of anger or out of embarrassment, but he is not working with us anymore. Each time we meet up on the street we look away, pretending we didn't see each other. Each time I remember him, I think *isn't this what racism does*?

Negotiations are proceeding with the kidnappers. The price has gone down to $100,000. There still is room to apply more pressure and lower the ransom. Ammar called his family and told them that he was fine. The kidnappers told his family that they won't hear his voice again unless they pay. Time is passing slowly and the issue requires a quick resolution. That is what everybody thinks. We will see tomorrow.

Faiza Al-Araji

THURSDAY, MARCH 4, 2004

My cousin Ammar (not the same Ammar mentioned in an earlier post by my mother), a 20-year old architect was driving to the University when someone shouted to him that he had a flat tire. When he stopped the car and got out to check, he found guns pointed at him and people asking him to get in a car with them. They left his car there and kidnapped him.

The next day the kidnappers called and demanded a $200,000 ransom. Eventually they settled for $20,000 and now Ammar is home safe.

Khalid Jarrar

MONDAY, MARCH 8, 2004

This week I received lots of e-mails. I would like to share a couple of them with you.

One was from an American woman whose 18-year old son just returned from Iraq. He said how impressed he was with the Iraqi people that he had the privilege to work with. He said he was especially impressed with the strong family bonds among the Iraqi people. He made many Iraqi friends and said he will remember them for life.

She went on to say that when her son told her he was going to Iraq, she was very afraid and frightened. She said that she was ignorant then of Muslim beliefs and traditions, but since her son has been in Iraq, she has learned a lot about Muslims. She said she has even read parts of the Qur'an to become more familiar with the culture and beliefs!

She has five other children, from ten to twenty-two years old. She said she cannot imagine the fears and the terrors that my children have had to witness. She knows as a mother that she would do all she could to protect her children. She hopes, God willing, that the terror and fear will soon give way to peace and calm in Iraq. She said she knows that Islam is a religion of peace just as her Christian religion, in its purest form, is one of peace. Sadly, people distort religion to satisfy their selfish whims.

She added that she is also a working mother, and she knows how very difficult it is to work and be a wife and mother at home. When her son was in Iraq it was very difficult to concentrate on her work but her family gave her comfort and peace and she trusted God to care for her soldier son. There are times when she said that she believed it would be better for mothers to control the government; then there might be peace and harmony.

She ended by saying that she wants me to know that I have many "sisters" in America who cry with me and pray that our families may soon know peace and security. A mother's heart is the same around the world; we weep for our children and for their future.

Another e-mail was sent to me, but it was addressed to Raed. This person said that with the horrific massacres in Karbala and Baghdad, we are now seeing the worst consequences of the illegal and immoral war led by the U.S. and the U.K. in Iraq. He believes that these events are part of a bigger plot aimed at starting a civil war in Iraq in order to partition it into small states. Divide and rule, he said. The colonialists/imperialists (U.S.A., U.K., and Israel) have organized this plot to balkanize Iraq in order to weaken it and keep control over it for decades to come.

He said that fortunately, from what we hear and read the Iraqis are aware of this and they are not going to allow such an evil plot to succeed. It is reassuring to see that Shias and Sunnis are sticking together.

He said that he lived in Baghdad in the 1970s and he knows how tolerant and respectful Iraqis are towards other religions. He believes that the occupiers are attempting to divide the Iraqi people along religious lines. He thinks it is vital that the Turkmen and Arabs unite in the North to keep Kirkuk from falling into the hands of Talabani, who he believes is a traitor to the Iraqi people. He also cited the Turkish press and relatives who live in Kirkuk that the Kurds are now selling big plots of land to Israelis in the Kurdish controlled areas, and has read that the U.S. has brought in hundreds of white South African mercenaries, and that the MOSSAD, CIA, and MI5 agents are now very active inside Iraq. It is to be hoped that the Iraqi patriots will succeed in eliminating these vermin.

Faiza Al-Araji

FRIDAY, MARCH 12, 2004

Azzam came back from his trip and brought many gifts from the delegates that took part in the Dubai conference that he attended. We enjoyed exploring them one by one, and tried to guess where each one came from: Iran? India? Pakistan? If there were small cooper cups or carved wood boxes, perhaps they were made in Ghana. If it was made of ceramic, maybe it came from China!

He brought small wood sculptures from the ex-U.S.S.R. countries, small handmade key holders from Sri Lanka, small Egyptian handmade rugs with the Sahara and camels depicted on them, and some small colorful pieces of carpet from Turkey.

His brother's wife called to invite us to lunch; it was Friday, the weekend holy day. We were speaking and laughing during lunch, but I couldn't stop the images in my memory.

We asked each other, "Do you remember the days of war? We came to your house running away from the American bombing at the airport, then the American forces came and surrounded your area too and we couldn't make it back home!" Everyone was laughing. Is it really a year now? Who can believe it? It seems like yesterday. Those events are still alive in our memories.

Here, in this kitchen, where the only light source was the smelly smoky gasoline lights, where we used to prepare meals, and lost between the sounds of American fighters and the Iraqi resistance, we tried our best to have a happy supper.

Near the kitchen, there is a small store room full of food rations and spare car parts; it was our shelter during the war. Early one

Saturday morning, we jumped from our beds terrified and rushed to the store room to hide with the bags of food. That was the first time we heard the noise of an American helicopter in Baghdad; we were shaking and wondering what the hell was going on. Some hours later the storm stopped and people went out to see what happened, and came back with different stories. But most of them said that the Americans pulled out their forces, and that streets were full of dead bodies of the Iraqi soldiers holding their Kalashnikovs. That was the first sign that Baghdad would soon fall.

We stayed at their house until the day Baghdad fell. There was an explosion nearby, and the children went upstairs and came down screaming, "Come and see! There are American tanks in the street!" We went to the roof shocked and frightened; there really were American tanks in the street. There were also soldiers wearing helmets and glasses, wearing American flags on their uniforms.

Majed shouted, "Raed, look! An American flag!"

Everything stopped at that moment. There was disappointment and sorrow mixed with happiness—happiness for the end of the war, but the feeling of pain is much greater than that of joy. The market in front of us was full of people, and the people there were ordered to raise their hands when they passed by an American tank. It was such embarrassing and humiliating event: American soldiers in their tanks and Iraqi civilians putting their hands up on their way back home.

Those days were full of sadness and pain that I can still feel in my heart now. I wish I could forget all of these memories right away.

Faiza Al-Araji

SATURDAY, MARCH 20, 2004

Good morning. Today is the first anniversary of the war against Iraq.

This morning on my way to work, I noticed there were no more soldiers in the streets, no Humvees, not a trace of American troops. That made me smile; it looks as thought they have suddenly disappeared. I think that's better for them and for us. If they are going to stay inside the military camps, it will be better and safer for them and for us. I hope this year everything will be better than the last year, especially for the security of the Iraqi people. I hope the economy will be better and give us a good chance to rehabilitate our country and our lives in the way that we believe we should.

Faiza Al-Araji

SUNDAY, MARCH 21, 2004

Hey Mom, this is Raed translating again. Happy Mother's Day. Happy Spring Festival Day. (But unfortunately a real sad occupation anniversary.)

Raed Jarrar

MONDAY, MARCH 22, 2004

Ahmad Yasin was killed today. I was planning to start blogging today, but I'm very sad and angry.

Raed Jarrar

TUESDAY, MARCH 23, 2004

Still studying, and translating my mother's blogs.

The hate and anger that the one can feel and see in the eyes of men explains why tragic events such September 11th can happen.

One year into the occupation of Iraq, and the "man of peace," as Bush called himself, decides to supervise personally the assassination plan against Ahmad Yasin. People were shouting in the demonstrations, here in Amman, and in Baghdad, Beirut, Cairo, Yemen, Damascus, and many other capitals. "We'll destroy Israel," they said, and I smiled.

I know they want to destroy Israel and kill Sharon, but I know that they can't. I don't know whether I'm supposed to cry or smile here. I feel sad, I know that all of this hate and anger because of the American position, and because of Israel's irresponsible acts, is going to be translated in one way or another in a bin Laden-like phenomenon.

I feel sleepy now. To be continued....

Raed Jarrar

WEDNESDAY, MARCH 24, 2004

Those who took the decision to start the war are still insisting that it was a sound choice; they read daily speeches to convince their people in their analyses and points of view. Why do they remind me of Saddam?

The main difference between them and Saddam is that he was dumber; he didn't make much of an effort to convince Iraqis of his ignorant foreign policy. But the American administration knows very well how to convince American people and take their blessings. Let's go back and discuss the reasons for starting this war.

There was a clear exaggeration in the real danger of Saddam and his weapons of mass destruction of which no one found any proof. Saddam Hussein was a real threat to his people, yes, but how could he cause any threat to the American people? The Bush administration tried its best to find any kind of relationship between Saddam and al-Qaeda, but it never did.

But they did convince the American taxpayers to start this war and cover the all expenses for the sake of protecting American citizens from any other terrorist attacks. No one can ignore how much Americans look up to and admire freedom; freedom for Americans is as sacred as God is for us. Americans don't mind sacrificing money and human lives to bring freedom to the people of Iraq, and Americans go to sleep happy, believing that their noble government is going to provide justice all over the world.

I wonder how many Americans believed in these slogans before the war, and how many of them changed their minds after? After one year of this war, I cannot see anything other than the war itself and the Americans occupying Iraq; no one has taken any further steps. All the indications say the Bush administration is not very interested in doing anything useful.

A few weeks ago, the Americans kicked out the president of Haiti and selected a new president. It was that simple! Everything happened quietly; the whole thing took just a couple of days.

It's just like what happened in Afghanistan: al-Qaeda bases were bombed, the Loya Jerga council was established, and everything was under control. American forces pulled out most of their soldiers from the cities and left some of them to guarantee security. We never hear anything about Afghanistan now. Why didn't they do the same in Iraq? Because each case has its special rules, and the case of Iraq is way too sophisticated and complicated. I won't mention Iraqi oil, but I'll consider it as a possibility.

The most complicated issue in the Middle East is the Palestinian crisis. This country, which thinks it is above international law, has weapons of mass destruction, yet it's the only country that the American administration protects.

And then there is Iran, the old enemy. And Syria, that stubborn country that refuses to surrender under pressure, and keeps minimum relationships with untouchable Israel. And there is Libya, which they exaggerate as usual in describing its threats, but we don't see in the Libyan model much more than what we saw in the Saddam model; lots of speeches and no action. So, occupying Iraq is giving the American administration a great base in the middle of the hottest region.

I want to add some things about Israel. Some people consider it the Eastern front of the United States. I see it as the ugly face of America. The democracy in Israel is just for the Israeli people, yet it's full of racism and aggression against its neighbors. It chooses violence as the only option in its foreign policy; is the Bush administration doing the same?

It is a real disaster to have a government convincing its people that their life, ambitions, and future cannot be achieved unless other countries and people are destroyed and killed. Isn't this the exact thing that Hitler stood for? Humiliate and kill other races because they are meant to be slaves to the masters? How did America react to Hitler at that time? Didn't the Americans considered him a sick obsessed person that would destroy humanity and joined World War II to destroy him?

Why did these values change now? Most of the financial support of the Hebron country comes from inside the United States, from Jews and other people with compassion for Israel. The entire region is going through a violent crisis full of assassinations and destruction, and the American reaction is either negative or neutral.

The aggressive mood and policy of Saddam Hussein was terrible, but so is the Israeli policy, if not worse! Why did the American administration consider Saddam as a threat to his neighbors and sacrifice so much to remove him, yet at the same time no one criticizes Israel's policies.

Don't the American people think about the paradox in their government's policies? I want an answer and I want it from the American people, not the American government. The American citizens pays taxes to the government, so the money can be used to launch deadly wars against other people, disfigure their history and their just struggle, using words like terrorism to create an atmosphere of hate.

The American citizen spends his whole week working hard to make sure he provides well for his family; he has friends, people whom he loves and worries about; he has ambitions and dreams; and then he has the weekend where he has fun with the rest of his family. But he rarely reads newspapers, and he doesn't really care about what is going on in the world, as long as he pays his taxes and trusts his government to do what's right for him. The American citizen doesn't even bother to check what his government is doing!

After the horrible events of 9/11, the world had to pay the price, and most of the price was paid by the Iraqi people. Why? What did we have to do with it? Maybe the U.S. administration was looking for a scapegoat and found that we are the best one available.

How many U.S. corporations were destroyed that day? Did the events really destroy the economy overnight or were there already problems with the economy and the attacks just brought it all to the surface? It takes a lot of money to get someone elected to office, and much of this money comes from a small percentage of the country: corporations. To these companies, elections are just a mere investment. When their candidate gets elected, their interests are served. Then these politicians start new wars and create new markets for the products made by these corporations: weapons, airplanes, cars, real estate. All they care about is themselves, not the American people, I mean, didn't these corporations have a clear interest in supporting Bush to start this war?

I wonder what will happen if Bush loses and Kerry becomes the president? Won't it be just the same for us? What's the difference between them? I don't think there's any significant difference, especially in foreign policy, because they have the same base of voters with the same demands who will vote only for their best interests. And I think it's not in the hands of Bush or Kerry personally; neither one of them puts the plans or the policies in place, they are just men with limited access. There's an administration that creates the plans and puts them into effect, controlling the fate of the American and Iraqi people—and the whole world—to serve a set of interests and priorities. They believe in it and agree upon it, and the people of the world know nothing of it. We spend many years of our lives arguing about what happened and what's going to happen, while a small elite group of people is controlling the fate of the world. Nothing will change until the people wake up, and the first to do so need to be the American people. But when?

I think it will happen when the American people exert enough pressure on the elections and force the government to enact campaign reform. They need to be rid of the lying and the propaganda.

If I were an American I'd set those as my priorities; that freedom is the right of my people and the people of every other country in the world. Every country's citizens are their own masters and live their lives in the best way that suits them, as long as they don't harm other people. There are no masters and slaves; people are all free and deserve equal opportunities in life. Being an American doesn't mean I have to be arrogant and self-centered or think that the world won't function right unless I intervene and program it as I like. I'd try to be more understanding of others' viewpoints. This would give me a sense of modesty and remove the barriers separating me from other people. I am not better than them. I'm never better than them, not for any reason.

Faiza Al-Araji

FRIDAY, MARCH 26, 2004

Happy news. The kidnapped boy was returned to his family last night. We will go to visit them after lunch to celebrate his safe return. His family paid 20,000 dinars. That was the final price. They received the money from the father at a predetermined place and hours later released Ammar. Upon his release the kidnappers kissed him and asked him to deliver greetings to his father. We saw Ammar in the evening; he looked good and was smiling. They didn't hurt him at all. He was held in a house outside Baghdad. He was locked up in a small room and was fed well. We didn't know if we should laugh or cry when we heard him talk about the kidnappers. In my heart I feel anxiety and fear. Who will stop these people. Who will be their next victim?

The weather is very warm in Baghdad. The summer has arrived suddenly. Some remains of cold might show up in the coming days. Then a short spring season will come. Then the summer will attack us, along with the electricity outages. Oh God! I don't even want to imagine that. I hope the electricity situation improves this summer. Today we will remove the carpets in the hallways. In the summer we remove all the carpets from the house including the dining room, the living room, and the bedrooms. Carpets are beautiful and give a warm look to the house, but the hot Baghdad weather makes us sacrifice this beauty in order to feel the cool tiles under our feet. I have also put away the heavy blankets, which I will wash and iron, and store in nylon bags on top of the closets until next year. God willing we will still be alive then.

Faiza Al-Araji

Here we go.

Another American veto, a controversial one.

And another meeting has been set for next month between Bush and Sharon.

Once upon a time, I wrote a blog attacking the new French law concerning religious symbols. I was totally against the idea of banning hijab; it was not because of what I think about hijab itself, it was because of the process and the theme of such a decision.

It's the classical how-to-do-it problem. I don't see anything wrong with the slogans of the Bush administration, maybe that's why I like to criticize them depending on what they say, not on what is imposed by their policies.

War on terror is the first priority? I agree with that. I'm a secular Muslim that fought against terrorism and fundamentalism for all of my life.

Democracy and freedom? No one would say no. It's not about catch phrases; it's about how to implement your ideas.

The foreign policy of the American administration is the main reason for global terrorism; was that a sharp statement full of buzz-words? Maybe.

The American foreign policy is putting people like me in a very weak position. Why? Because in extreme circumstances, extreme ideologies rule and dominate. And I am, unfortunately, not an extremist.

The global political environment is directly controlled by the United States government; it happens that they are the superpower, and they are the ones responsible for this extremely tense time we are all going through.

It is the right of everyone to wonder whether American foreign policy decision makers are doing the right thing or not. Is it their right to protect their interests? Yes, it is.

But the don't think of their interests vs. the rest of the world's interests. Why give us the slogans of one world, one village? Just act like the Roman Empire, and occupy our countries.

Why am I wearing my jeans? Why did I have my lunch at Burger King today? Why does the voice of Avril Lavigne feel so familiar to me? Why do we all use the same Nokia and the same Compaq? And why do we all like Mexican tequila? Is it because these things are a part of the American world? Or is it because they are the details of *our* world?

I mean it's a very simple thing to clarify: do you—Americans— want to rule the world? Or do you want to help us all build our civilization? Do you really want to know why terrorism is gaining deeper and stronger roots? Do you want to know how terrorism "justifies" and "rationalizes" its goals and methodologies? Bomb more countries using your depleted uranium bullets searching for their WMD. Kill more civilians and destroy their culture to defend their right to freedom. Assassinate more political leaders, ask for political solutions, and give the world more examples of how a great veto can protect killers.

Who are terrorists? People like us: depressed and frustrated, those who have lost faith in international law, who are being killed and injured in Palestine and Iraq and Lebanon. Do you think the answer for such a problem is attacking them? Do you really think the war on terrorism is a war of missiles and tanks?

What is the difference between Bush and bin Laden? Both are violent extremists that can kill!

Shouldn't a president like Bush reflect the ideologies of a rational community, a community that is based on "civilized" citizens? A community that believes in the authority of law? How do you treat a killer in New York? Kill him without a trial? How do you treat a thief in Washington? Cut off his hands? Where did this ethics of violence and jungle-rules come from? Is there a time when the American administration (the one with bigger tanks, faster fighters, and the most powerful weapons of mass destruction) will understand the real war they are starting?

It is the war of cultures.

Raed Jarrar

MONDAY, MARCH 29, 2004

The Arab summit. What the hell? Who cares? Just show me a single Arab that is expecting anything to come out from these unfruitful-since-ever meetings. Postpone the summit, change the time and place! It's a free world, dudes. The only interesting thing was the Israeli reaction that considered the event of postponing the summit as a great development in the Arab world!

It's now, and just now, that I feel proud of my progressive world. Stop, change topic, reload, fire. Oh boy, I'm thinking seriously about starting a new blog for hate mails. I discovered some hate comments sites too; you can find creative comments such as:

"I have read your mothers blog. I think it will kill her to have pieces of her children delivered to her in plastic garbage bags."

I'm sure my mother won't be happy to receive pieces of me in a bag whether it was a plastic or a paper one. But that was artistic though.

Topic of the day: How can we hate each other?

I'm not very good at this, but I'll try. I don't like my ex-fiancé because she stole four years of my life. I don't like my ex-friend because he stole eight years and five thousand bucks. That's my hate list. I don't hate them much though. I miss them sometimes. Okay, I don't like my cat from time to time, too. That's it! The end.

But how can anyone *hate* someone without even meeting him? This remarkable phenomenon of hate mails is more than the mistake of one arrogant individual; this is a result of a well designed "Hate the Other" policy.

Hint of the day: I think a motto like, "You are either with us or against us," would be great to start any "Hate the Other" campaign. When our governments (the Saddam government, the Bush government, etc.) put all the pressure they can to use the media as a public orientation device, and keep on repeating the same slogans, lies, and stories in a long-term brainwash procedure, what do they expect as a result?

They aim to redefine the meaning of some key words, nationality is one of them: if you are a good citizen, you must *love* your country, be flexible enough to understand any kind of sacrifice, and at the same time you should hate all things coming from other worlds. Governments teach us that our culture is *the* culture, our language is *the* supreme one, our traditions are *the* best, our ethics, our flag, our weather, our...our...our....

Hate the other. Be completely suspicious all the time—even with your fellow citizens. Maybe they like foreign ideas, maybe they are controlled by the bad people, or maybe they are betrayers. Attack the other. Don't ever listen to what he might say. Usually there are certain predefined titles to categorize your enemy: Zionist, Ba'athist, Communist, Imperialist, Terrorist, Islamist; these are small soundproof boxes that you must put your enemy inside, and you'll never hear his poisoning ideologies. Can and dump.

The real question is not whether our governments are going to change their ways or not. The real question is about ourselves; are we going to buy their stories? Are we going to drown in this sea of hatred? Are we going to build new walls between our cultures?

It is *your* right to be different; it is *my* right, too. But it's *our* right to live in peace.

Raed Jarrar

ABOUT THE AUTHORS

Faiza Al-Araji

Faiza Al-Araji is a civil engineer and worked as the executive manager for the family's water treatment firm in Baghdad. At the start of the war, she began working with local Iraqi non-governmental organizations to assist people with food and medicine.

Due to the deterioration of the security situation in Iraq, Faiza and her family moved to Amman, Jordan, in December, 2004 where she has continued her humanitarian activities by voluntarily organizing campaigns to collect funds to help Iraqi refugees with food and medical supplies.

Faiza attended conferences in Malaysia and Italy in 2007, at which she discussed the ramifications of the invasion and subsequent occupation from her experiences as an Iraqi woman. She also participated in the 2005 SIT Peace Building Institute in Vermont, and has toured the United States as part of the delegation of Iraqi woman invited by the GX organization and testified before Congress about the disastrous situation in Iraq.

She is currently working with a local Jordanian non-governmental organization as Project Coordinator to improve education for Iraqi women and children living in Jordan. Faiza maintained two blogs during the war, *The War Diary* and *A Family in Baghdad*, on which parts of this book are based.

Raed Jarrar

Raed Jarrar is an Iraqi political analyst currently based in Washington, DC. A professional architect, Jarrar obtained his first degree from the University of Baghdad in 2000. Jarrar continued postgraduate studies at the University of Jordan in Amman, Jordan where he researched community based post war reconstruction in Iraq.

After the U.S.-led invasion, Jarrar returned home to become country director for CIVIC Worldwide, the only door-to-door casualty survey group in post war Iraq. He then established Emaar, (meaning "reconstruction" in Arabic), a grassroots organization that coordinated with political leadership and civil society throughout Iraq in order to rebuild Iraqi civil society and physical infrastructure. Emaar successfully implemented hundreds of community based projects with minimal funding.

In 2005, Jarrar moved to California and continued to contribute to a series of Iraq related projects. On the environment, he worked as consultant and translator for UNEP Japan to preserve Iraqi marshlands.

Jarrar has acted as political analyst and interpreter for a UNDP Iraq sponsored conference in South Africa on the Truth and Reconciliation Commission. He canvassed door to door with California Peace Action to solicit support for an initiative urging Congress to outlaw the maintenance of permanent U.S. military bases in Iraq.

Most recently, Jarrar became the Iraq Consultant for the American Friends Service Committee (AFSC) in Washington, DC. Jarrar endeavors to advance discourse between Iraqi leaders and members of the U.S. Congress. To that end, he has organized a series of meetings between U.S. and Iraqi officials and helped facilitate the publication of numerous policy papers and op-eds by Iraqi leaders in prominent U.S. newspapers. In addition, Raed Jarrar is a contributing writer and analyst for *Foreign Policy in Focus* and *AlterNet*.

Jarrar has appeared on various news channels, including *CNN, CNN Intl, Al Jazeera, Al Alam, BBC,* and *Democracy Now*. Several radio stations including member stations of *NPR, BBC, CBC, CBS, FOX,* and *Pacifica* have engaged his expertise and his analyses have been published in numerous newspapers. Jarrar maintains *Raed in the Middle*, a widely read web log (on which portions of this book are based), dedicated to a timely analysis of current Iraqi political conditions.

Khalid Jarrar

Khalid Jarrar is a 25 year-old environmental engineer, who lived in Baghdad until he was forced to leave in July 2005. A media activist, he has worked with several non-governmental and media organizations since 2003.

Khalid also maintains a blog, *Tell Me A Secret*, and has been hosted on major and small media outlets in interviews and political programs throughout the world. He has produced a series of documentaries about Iraq for the *CBC*, which were well-received audiences. Khalid now lives in Amman, Jordan, with his parents and Tigger the cat.